High

GATEWAY TO

GERMAN LIEDER

*An Anthology of German Song
and Interpretation*

John Glenn Paton

Cover photo: The Golden Gate at Herrenhausen Garden,
Hanover, Germany

Alfred

ISBN   0-7390-0106-X (Book)
ISBN   0-7390-0107-8 (Book & CD)
ISBN   0-7390-0108-6 (CD)

Table of Contents

Introduction. 4

The Composers 6

The Poets 10

Lieder

Ludwig van Beethoven

    1. Die Ehre Gottes aus der Natur (Gellert) 13

    2. Nur wer die Sehnsucht kennt (Goethe) 16

    3. Aus Goethe's Faust (Es war einmal ein König) (Goethe) 19

Carl Loewe

    4. Mädchen sind wie der Wind (Anonymous) 25

    5. Süßes Begräbnis (Rückert) 29

Franz Schubert

    6. Das Rosenband (Klopstock) 34

    7. Seligkeit (Hölty) 37

    8. An die Nachtigall (Claudius) 41

    9. Der Tod und das Mädchen (Claudius) 43

    10. An die Musik (Schober) 46

    11. Lachen und Weinen (Rückert) 49

    12. Ständchen (Rellstab) 53

Fanny Mendelssohn Hensel

    13. Nachtwanderer (Eichendorff) 59

    14. Kommen und Scheiden (Lenau) 64

Felix Mendelssohn

    15. Jagdlied (Des Knaben Wunderhorn) 69

    16. Auf Flügeln des Gesanges (Heine) 75

    17. Nachtlied (Eichendorff) 81

Robert Schumann

    18. Widmung (Rückert) 85

    19. Der Nussbaum (Mosen) 90

    20. Die Lotosblume (Heine) 96

    21. In der Fremde (Eichendorff) 99

    22. Ein Jüngling liebt ein Mädchen (Heine). 103

    23. Du Ring an meinem Finger (Chamisso) 106

    24. Nachtlied (Goethe) 111

Franz Liszt

    25. Du bist wie eine Blume (Heine) 113

Josephine Lang

    26. An die Entfernte (Lenau) 116

Robert Franz

    27. Aus meinen großen Schmerzen (Heine) 120

    28. Im Herbst (Müller) 123

Clara Schumann

    29. Liebst du um Schönheit (Rückert) 128

Peter Cornelius

    30. Ein Ton (Cornelius) 133

Johannes Brahms

    31. Die Mainacht (Hölty) 137

    32. Wiegenlied (Des Knaben Wunderhorn) 143

    33. O kühler Wald (Brentano) 146

    34. Vergebliches Ständchen (Zuccalmaglio) 150

    35. Sapphische Ode (Schmidt) 156

    36. Wir wandelten (Daumer) 160

    37. Wie Melodien zieht es mir (Groth) 165

Hugo Wolf

    38. Der Gärtner (Mörike) 169

    39. Fußreise (Mörike) 173

    40. Das verlassene Mägdlein (Mörike) 180

    41. Gesang Weyla's (Mörike) 184

    42. Anakreon's Grab (Goethe) 187

    43. In dem Schatten meiner Locken (Geibel) 191

    44. Auch kleine Dinge (Heyse) 196

Richard Strauss

    45. Die Nacht (Gilm) 199

    46. Allerseelen (Gilm) 203

    47. All mein Gedanken, mein Herz und mein Sinn (Dahn) 208

    48. Du meines Herzens Krönelein (Dahn) 212

IPA Symbols for German 216

Introduction

The 48 lieder contained here are only a sampling of the wonderful world of German art songs. I hope that this book is a *Gateway to German Lieder* in the sense of giving access to a realm of imagination and expression created by some of the greatest composers ever known.

This book brings together various kinds of information that would otherwise require research in various books. The commentary pages that precede the songs will help the singer especially with the preparatory steps that should precede actual singing: translating the text, analyzing its meaning, reciting it with correct and expressive diction, and researching the relevant historical background. The goal is artistic communication with an audience, based on the singer's clear understanding of the message and meaning of the song.

German tempo and style markings are translated on the pages where they are used. Tempos in Romantic style are never absolute and never metronomic, but metronome markings are provided as a starting point. Where the composer did not give a metronome marking, I have given one in a footnote, clearly designated as a suggestion and marked with "ca." to indicate that it is approximate at best.

Composers seldom provided full instructions for phrasing and breathing. Aside from breathing at rests, most songs contain situations where the singer must cut a note short in order to breathe and begin the next phrase on time. We must take in air for physical reasons, but from the singer's point of view it is even more important to make the poem and the musical line clear and expressive, in other words, to articulate the musical line.

Some written punctuation signs stand for breaths but others do not. One must read the poem aloud to sense the differentiation. I have inserted two kinds of phrase markings above the vocal line:

1) ∨ , where the musical line must be interrupted in order to articulate the text correctly;

2) ❜ , where a breath may be taken if it is needed for physical comfort.

Most of the songs contained here were thoroughly researched when they appeared in editions of great composers' complete works in the late 1800s. Many such editions were published by Breitkopf und Haertel in Leipzig and are available in modern reprints in major libraries. In view of this, I did not feel that it was necessary for me to travel to see all of the manuscripts and first editions that are listed in this book as "Sources." The same is true of the listed sources of poems, which are either the first editions or later editions that I have been able to consult or both. Many poems were published in periodicals before they appeared in books; only a few of these sources were available to me.

As we prepare to interpret these beautiful songs for our audiences, our two best guides are accurate information, such as described above, and our own honest musical impulses. Some singers believe that there is a "tradition" of performance that they must learn, but this is only partly true. A comparison of recordings made of any particular song by German singers since 1900 will reveal that performance styles have changed considerably with the generations. Furthermore, great singers have always put their individual stamp onto whatever they sang.

Most students benefit from listening to recordings made by established artists, but some recorded performances contain interpretive effects, even distortions, that are effective only when done by the particular artist who originated them. The best safeguard against this problem is to listen to multiple recordings of the same songs, not accepting any one recording as a final authority. By hearing several interpretations, the singer is set free to discover a personal one that is not an imitation of another singer.

Coordinated with this book are two CDs containing all of the piano accompaniments, artistically recorded by Joan Thompson, pianist, under my close supervision. We aimed to record the accompaniments both expressively and faithfully to the composers' wishes. We tried to avoid expressive choices that would mislead a singer to adopt any extremes of interpretation.

The biographical notes about composers include references to books that contain enlightening information about those individuals. In addition, several books contain invaluable information about many composers and their lieder. To the singer who wants to research other songs, I recommend these books and acknowledge my indebtedness to them:

Singer and Accompanist: The Performance of Fifty Songs by Gerald Moore. New York: Macmillan, 1954.

The Ring of Words by Philip L. Miller. Garden City: Doubleday, 1963.

The German Lied and Its Poetry by Elaine Brody and Robert A. Fowkes. New York: New York University, 1971.

Reclams Liedführer by Werner Oehlmann. Stuttgart: Philipp Reclam, 1973.

The Nineteenth-Century German Lied by Lorraine Gorrell. Portland: Amadeus, 1993.

Poetry into Song: Performance and Analysis of Lieder by Deborah Stein and Robert Spillman. Oxford: Oxford University, 1996.

Few authors can say that they write a book alone. I gratefully acknowledge constant support, encouragement and editorial contributions from Joan Thompson, my wife. Dr. Ann Paton, my sister, also made valuable suggestions. Among the talented professionals at the Alfred Publishing Company, I would like to acknowledge editorial assistance from Sonya Sardon, as well as the skillful engraving by Greg Plumblee, masterful layout design by Bruce Goldes, and art direction by Holly Fraser.

If this *Gateway* is successful, it will awaken young singers' curiosity and provide some of the necessary tools to explore more songs in German, for instance: pre-Romantic songs by Albert, Haydn, Schulz, Mozart and Zelter; other Romantic composers, including Wagner; and post-Romantic songs by Mahler, Reger, Pfitzner, Hindemith and Reutter. The rewards will be great.

John Glenn Paton
Los Angeles, California

The Composers

(in chronological order by year of birth)

Great poets put a little of themselves into each poem, and great composers put a little of themselves into each song. While learning a song, the singer may be curious to learn more about its creators. The aim of the following pages is to encourage that curiosity by supplying basic information that focuses on a singer's interests. To learn more about composers the best starting point is always *The New Grove Dictionary of Music and Musicians*, edited by Stanley Sadie [London: Macmillan, 1980, 20 volumes]. In addition, there are good biographies of most composers and poets. Some other books devoted exclusively to lieder are also mentioned below.

Ludwig van Beethoven (Bonn, 1770 – Vienna, 1827)

Beethoven wrote a great deal of vocal music, including the opera *Fidelio* and various choral works, but he is now revered more for his symphonies, piano works and chamber music. Songs were not as marketable for Beethoven as they were later, when pianos and home music-making became more common. Nevertheless, his more than 70 songs have a musical originality and significance that far surpasses the songs even of Haydn and Mozart. Beethoven's *An die ferne Geliebte*, a cycle of six songs joined together into one continuous movement, is both a bold experiment and a masterpiece.

Beethoven lived in Vienna after 1792, and by 1800 he knew that his hearing was failing. When he wrote the lieder in this book, Beethoven's hearing had failed considerably but he was still able to perform in public as a pianist. During 1805–1814 he was concerned about *Fidelio* and its various revisions.

Songs: "*Die Ehre Gottes aus der Natur*," 13
"*Nur wer die Sehnsucht kennt*," 16
"*Aus Goethe's Faust*," 19

Carl Loewe (Lobjühn, near Halle, 1796 – Kiel, 1869)

Loewe earned his early musical education by singing as a choirboy in Halle, Germany. He witnessed the incursion of Swedish, Russian and Prussian troops who were driving Napoleon's armies back to France in 1813. On one occasion he and a friend were robbed of their money, shoes and outer clothing by two armed and mounted Cossacks. After peace was restored, Loewe received scholarships to study theology at the University of Halle, and partially supported himself by giving piano lessons.

Loewe served as music director and teacher at a seminary in Stettin, which became his home for the rest of his life. His first wife, Julie, died after five years of marriage, and in 1826 he married Auguste, a talented singer who often sang his songs in public. Loewe's autobiography shows a gift for storytelling. In German speaking countries Loewe remains famous for his ballads, narrative songs that sometimes reached a great length.

Songs: "*Mädchen sind wie der Wind*," 25
"*Süßes Begräbnis*," 29

Franz Schubert (Vienna, 1797 – 1828)

Schubert received his early and thorough musical training while he was a choirboy with the imperial court chapel. Later he rejected teaching school for a living and lived as a free artist, which in his case meant relative poverty. Friends helped him, but he was not a brilliant performer and therefore did not attract any wealthy patron.

When Schubert died before his 32nd birthday, an obituary stated that he had written as many as 200 songs. The true number is over 600. Schubert wrote prolifically in several genres, including operas, symphonies, chamber music and piano music. He did not always date his compositions and in many cases produced several works with identical titles.

Indispensable for Schubert research is the thematic catalog compiled by O. E. Deutsch, who cataloged and numbered Schubert's works as nearly as possible in the order he wrote them. "*Das Rosenband*," D. 280, for instance, is approximately the 280th piece of music that Schubert composed (about half of those were songs), even though he was only 18 at the time. To appreciate Schubert's creative energy, one should remember that an entire symphony or opera receives only one "Deutsch number" and the numbers run to 998. (An older edition of the Deutsch catalog is available in English. The newest revision exists only in German.)

Many books have been written and still are being written about Schubert's songs. Three that are comprehensive and useful: (1) *Schubert's Songs* by Richard Capell [London, 1928, revised by M. Cooper, 1973]; (2) *Schubert's Songs* by Dietrich Fischer-Dieskau, translated by K. S. Whitton [New York: Limelight Editions, 1984]; (3) *Schubert Song Companion* by John Reed [Manchester: Mandolin, 1985].

Songs: "*Das Rosenband*," 34
"*Seligkeit*," 37
"*An die Nachtigall*," 41
"*Der Tod und das Mädchen*," 43
"*An die Musik*," 46
"*Lachen und Weinen*," 49
"*Ständchen*," 53

Fanny Mendelssohn Hensel (Hamburg, 1805 – Berlin, 1847)

Fanny Mendelssohn Hensel was the oldest of four siblings in the intellectually gifted Mendelssohn family. She and her brother Felix both studied piano and composition from an early age. Being older, she was Felix's musical advisor for as long as he lived at home. Fanny offered no open rebellion to her father's decision that she was not to perform in public or pursue a musical career. She had a happy marriage with Wilhelm Hensel, official painter to the Prussian court. Her biweekly Sunday morning concerts at home drew elegant audiences; every important musician who visited Berlin met the Mendelssohns. She died of a stroke during a rehearsal for one of her concerts.

As Fanny Hensel's music is being rediscovered, we are learning that her musical language was much more chromatic than that of her brother. Most of her over 200 songs are still unpublished. Some may be found in *16 Songs by Fanny Mendelssohn Hensel*, edited by John Glenn Paton, Alfred Publishing Co., 1995.

Songs: *"Nachtwanderer,"* 59
  "Kommen und Scheiden," 64

Felix Mendelssohn (Hamburg, 1809 – Leipzig, 1847)

Felix Mendelssohn and his sister Fanny were trained in the conservative song tradition by Carl Friedrich Zelter, who favored strophic songs with simple accompaniments. Felix had his wealthy family's support in finding a career: he traveled in Italy, France and England before making a conscious choice to live in Germany as a German musician. By conducting their works, he helped to make Bach and Handel famous in Germany.

Mendelssohn and Schumann mutually influenced each other's creative work during 1835–40, when they both lived in Leipzig. Mendelssohn had immense energy and he generously promoted the careers of other worthy musicians. He had many talents: he drew well and painted watercolors, spoke several languages and was a prolific letter writer. He composed about 100 solo songs with piano in addition to duets and choral works.

Mendelssohn had a happy marriage that resulted in five children. He died only a few months after his sister Fanny and of a similar stroke.

Songs: *"Jagdlied,"* 69
  "Auf Flügeln des Gesanges," 75
  "Nachtlied," 81

Robert Schumann (Zwickau, 1810 – Endenich, near Bonn, 1856)

In his youth, Schumann improvised at the piano and wrote fantastical prose. He wrote a letter of admiration to Schubert but did not send it. After news came of Schubert's death, Schumann was heard sobbing during the following night.

At age 18 Schumann began to study piano with Friedrich Wieck and met his daughter Clara, aged nine. He had other loves during the next years, but as Clara grew up she and Robert fell in love. Their struggle to overcome Wieck's objections constitutes one of the great love stories of music history.

Schumann's first published compositions were 23 opus numbers of piano music that developed an innovative pianistic style. In 1840 he turned to writing lieder and produced 138 songs that incorporated his new way of writing for the keyboard. Also in that year Clara turned 21, and the impatient lovers married.

Schumann was not a public performer, but he founded a musical magazine, *Neue Zeitschrift für Musik* (New Magazine for Music). In its pages he introduced new composers to the German public, notably Chopin, Franz and Brahms.

During his career Schumann published 245 songs, but the finest were those of 1840, called his "song year." In later years there were signs of declining inspiration and periods of depression. After a suicide attempt in 1854, Schumann stayed in a private asylum until he died.

Valuable books for singers include: (1) *The Songs of Robert Schumann* by Eric Sams [New York: Norton, 1969, revised 1975]; (2) *The Singer's Schumann* by Thilo Reinhard [New York: Pelion, 1989].

Songs: *"Widmung,"* 85
  "Der Nussbaum," 90
  "Die Lotosblume," 96
  "In der Fremde," 99
  "Ein Jüngling liebt ein Mädchen," 103
  "Du Ring an meinem Finger," 106
  "Nachtlied," 111

Franz Liszt (Raiding, near Sopron, Hungary, 1811 – Bayreuth, 1886)

Born to a Hungarian father and a German mother, Liszt showed such early talent that his family moved to Vienna for his training. There he studied with Antonio Salieri, as did Schubert, and met Schubert and Beethoven. At age 11 he was studying further in Paris, and at 12 he ended a triumphant London concert by improvising on themes given to him from the audience.

Liszt became the greatest piano virtuoso of his age, but he was also an innovative composer and an advocate for new music. He used his power as a performer to introduce new works by many composers. He popularized songs by Schubert and others by transcribing them for piano and playing the transcriptions on his recitals.

Although he is usually remembered as a composer for the piano, Liszt published 72 songs in Italian, French, German, Hungarian and English.

Song: *Du bist wie eine Blume,"* 113

Josephine Lang (Munich, 1815 – Tübingen, 1880)

Josephine Lang was the granddaughter, daughter and niece of professional sopranos. During his visits to Munich, Mendelssohn gave her counterpoint lessons, as he reported at length in a letter to his sisters, October 6, 1831: "When she sings the first tone with her gentle voice, every person becomes still and meditative, touched through and through . . . I teach her what she already knows instinctively." Although Mendelssohn did not want his sister's compositions published, he encouraged Lang to publish because she needed money.

Lang married Christian Reinhold Köstlin and wrote many songs on his poems, written under the name C. Reinhold. After her husband died, Lang had to support their six children. One of her daughters, Maria Fellinger, was a friend to Brahms later in Vienna.

Song: "*An die Entfernte*," 116

Robert Franz (Halle, 1815 – 1892)

Franz spent almost all of his life in Halle and was largely self-taught. He became an organist and choir director, married and had three children. Schumann encouraged Franz, and Liszt wrote a book about him. Franz wrote piano accompaniments for works of Bach and Handel for the editions of their complete works. He was greatly honored in his time, but experienced the sorrow of losing his hearing by age 52.

Franz published 279 lieder and a number of choral works.

Songs: "*Aus meinen großen Schmerzen*," 120
"*Im Herbst*," 123

Clara Schumann (Leipzig, 1819 – Frankfurt, 1896)

Clara Schumann was first acclaimed internationally as the brilliant pianist Clara Wieck, daughter and student of Friedrich Wieck. A rigorously serious artist, she was the first pianist to play entire Beethoven sonatas in public concerts (Vienna, 1839), instead of limiting herself to short selections.

Her father's plans for her career were ruined when Clara fell in love with his former student, Robert Schumann. Clara and Robert married on September 12, 1840. As a composer she had already published 11 opus numbers of piano music, including a concerto. Robert wanted her to continue to compose, but his composing and her household duties came first. Years of amazing exertion followed: Clara bore eight children within 14 years, ran the household, concertized widely and taught at the Leipzig Conservatory.

Johannes Brahms entered the Schumanns' lives in 1853; he was Clara's mainstay as she underwent the tragedy of Robert's insanity. Clara's concert tours supported her large family. She became ever more influential as a teacher and performed until 1891.

Song: "*Liebst du um Schönheit*," 128

Peter Cornelius (Mainz, 1824 – 1874)

Cornelius was the son of two actors and had many talents; he both acted and played the violin professionally. He attracted friends among the leading poets and musicians of his time both in Berlin and in the circle around Franz Liszt at Weimar. He later taught in Munich and belonged to Wagner's close circle of friends, but he managed to avoid becoming a mere imitator of Wagner. He wrote two successful operas, many choral works and at least 78 songs. His strong Catholic faith comes forth in a set of nine songs based on the Lord's Prayer and in his *Christmas Songs*.

Song: "*Ein Ton*," 133

Johannes Brahms (Hamburg, 1833 – Vienna, 1897)

Brahms grew up in poverty; in his teens he played the piano in waterfront bars. At age 20 Brahms toured with a Hungarian violinist who introduced him to another violinist, Joseph Joachim, who became Brahms's best friend. Joachim sent Brahms to the Schumanns, who embraced him with enthusiasm. Six months later Robert Schumann was hospitalized and Brahms became Clara's chief source of practical and emotional support. Clara was 14 years older than Brahms. He fell in love with her, but how she responded is not known because they both destroyed written communications from that time. Later, they lived in different cities but remained close friends and musical advisors to each other. Brahms fell in love with various other women but never married.

Brahms was an excellent pianist but no showman. He held various conducting posts and continued to perform until royalties from his compositions enabled him to live comfortably. He destroyed many compositions that did not satisfy him, as well as most of the preliminary sketches of works that he published. He published 194 songs for solo voice and piano, as well as duets, two songs with viola and 121 arrangements of German folk songs.

Brahms studied Schubert's songs assiduously. He said that he learned from Schubert to put very few expression marks in the voice part.

Brahms lived the latter half of his life in Vienna, but traveled often. He was often brusque and unthinking toward his best friends; there were even quarrels and reconciliations with Joachim and Clara Schumann. But he could also be charming, and throughout his life there were friends ready to help him out of regard for his greatness as a musician. He died of liver cancer.

Invaluable information is found in: (1) *Brahms's Lieder* by Max Friedlaender, translated by C. Leonard Leese [London: Oxford University Press, 1928]; (2) *A Guide to the Solo Songs of Johannes Brahms* by Lucien Stark [Bloomington: Indiana University, 1995]; (3) *Brahms: The*

Vocal Music by A. Craig Bell [London: London University Presses, 1996].

Songs: *"Die Mainacht,"* 137
      "Wiegenlied," 143
      "O kühler Wald," 146
      "Vergebliches Ständchen," 150
      "Sapphische Ode," 156
      "Wir wandelten," 160
      "Wie Melodien zieht es mir," 165

Hugo Wolf

(Windischgraz, now Slovenj Gradec, Slovenia, 1860 – Vienna, 1903)
Wolf had a Slovenian mother and a German father. When Wolf rebelled against school, his parents sent him to Vienna to live with an aunt and study music. At age 15 he showed his first compositions to Wagner, whose kindness made Wolf a lifelong devotee. After he was dismissed from the Conservatory for breaches of discipline, Wolf was assisted by friends who perceived his talent. He had no regular income and lived in poverty. Gustav Mahler was one of his roommates for a time. Most of his songs were composed in temporary lodgings where friends allowed him to stay free.

Wolf disliked teaching; his best source of income was writing music criticism for a newspaper. He was assertively pro-Wagner and anti-Brahms; his stinging criticisms alienated certain musicians who later refused him when he needed their help.

Wolf's *Italian Serenade* for string quartet is often performed; otherwise, all of his music has been forgotten except the songs. He published 245 songs and left another 103 unpublished, some of them destroyed. His most typical method of working was to immerse himself in a single volume of poetry, composing in an intense state of concentration until his inspiration ran out.

Wolf's achievement was to apply Wagner's musical-dramatic methods to the lied, dramatizing and intensifying the poem with motivically based music. He set words to music with unprecedented sensitivity, sometimes resulting in startling dramatic miniatures.

Late in 1897, Wolf was overtaken by mental illness traceable to syphilis. The next year he entered an asylum where he stayed until his death.

Singers should consult: (1) *The Songs of Hugo Wolf* by Eric Sams [London, 1961, revised 1981]; (2) *Hugo Wolf: The Vocal Music* by Susan Youens [Princeton: Princeton University, 1992].

Songs: *"Der Gärtner,"* 169
      "Fußreise," 173
      "Das verlassene Mägdlein," 180
      "Gesang Weyla's," 184
      "Anakreon's Grab," 187
      "In dem Schatten meiner Locken," 191
      "Auch kleine Dinge," 196

Richard Strauss (Munich, 1864–Garmisch, 1949)

Strauss was born to wealth through his mother, who belonged to the Pschorr brewing family. He was born to music through his father, Franz Strauss, the principal horn player in the Munich Court Orchestra for 49 years. Franz Strauss detested Wagner and his music but could not keep his son from the influence of Wagner's music dramas.

Strauss performed publicly as a pianist and, much more significantly, as a conductor. In 1894 he married a prominent dramatic soprano, Pauline de Ahna. The Strausses performed many lieder recitals together. Many of Strauss's finest songs were written long before his first operatic successes, *Salome, Elektra* and *Der Rosenkavalier*. In old age he had great difficulties with the Nazi government: he resisted their anti-Jewish policies when he could, but he cooperated with them to protect his Jewish daughter-in-law and her children.

Between the ages of 6 and 83 Strauss composed just over 200 lieder, many of them in two versions, with piano and with orchestra. His last masterpiece was the set of songs known as *Vier letzte Lieder* (Four Last Songs, 1948). Strauss differed from all earlier composers in this book in that he wrote primarily for professional singers performing in public, rather than amateurs singing at home, perhaps with no audience at all. Because of this difference in approach, songs by Strauss, even the quieter ones, have a theatrical quality that is not typical of lieder in general.

Singers should consult: (1) *Ton und Wort: The Lieder of Richard Strauss* by Barbara A. Peterson. [Ann Arbor: UMI Research, 1980]. (2) *Richard Strauss: A Critical Commentary on His Life and Works* by Norman Del Mar [Ithaca: Cornell University, 1986, 3 volumes.].

Songs: *"Die Nacht,"* 199
      "Allerseelen," 203
      "All mein Gedanken, mein Herz
        und mein Sinn," 208
      "Du meines Herzens Krönelein," 212

The Poets

(in chronological order by year of birth)

Anonymous, from **Des Knaben Wunderhorn**

(The Boy's Magic Horn, 1805)
This is the designation of various old German poems that were collected, partly re-written and published by Arnim and Brentano. The first sizable collection of German folk poems, *Wunderhorn* was Gustav Mahler's source for some of his finest orchestral lieder and symphonic movements with vocal soloists.

> Mendelssohn, *"Jagdlied,"* 69
> Brahms, *"Wiegenlied,"* 143

Christian Fürchtegott Gellert

(Hainichen, 1715 – Leipzig, 1769)
Gellert studied in Leipzig while J. S. Bach still directed the church music there. Gellert became a professor of poetry, rhetoric and morality at the University of Leipzig. He successfully reached many readers by expressing his moral and religious messages in fiction, comedies and versified fables.

> Beethoven, *"Die Ehre Gottes aus der Natur,"* 13

Friedrich Gottlieb Klopstock

(Quedlinburg, 1724 – Hamburg, 1803)
Klopstock is credited with introducing elements of personal feeling that had been missing from earlier German poetry. He was highly regarded for his epic poem on the theme of salvation, *Der Messias* (Messiah).

> Schubert, *"Das Rosenband,"* 34

Matthias Claudius

(Reinfeld, Holstein, 1740 – Hamburg, 1815)
Claudius was a popular poet in his time, printing his finest poems in the newspaper he had founded.

> Schubert, *"An die Nachtigall,"* 41
> Schubert, *"Der Tod und das Mädchen,"* 43

Ludwig Christoph Heinrich Hölty

(Mariensee, near Hanover, 1748 – 1776).
As a student in Göttingen, Hölty was a founding member of a literary circle called the *Hainbund* (grove-union) made up of fervent admirers of Klopstock. Schubert used more than 30 poems by Hölty, and Brahms used six. All of these were the altered versions made by J. H. Voss.

> Schubert, *"Seligkeit,"* 37
> Brahms, *"Die Mainacht,"* 137

Johann Wolfgang von Goethe

(Frankfurt am Main, 1749 – Weimar, 1832).
One can hardly express the significance of Goethe to German culture. In addition to writing plays that rival those of Shakespeare, he also wrote lyric poetry, novels that have been translated into every major language, scientific studies and philosophical essays. Educated in law, he filled administrative posts for the Duke of Weimar for 57 years from 1775 until his death. Because of these responsibilities each of his major works was written over a period of years.

> Beethoven, *"Nur wer die Sehnsucht kennt,"* 16
> Beethoven, *"Aus Goethe's Faust,"* 19
> R. Schumann, *"Nachtlied,"* 111
> Wolf, *"Anakreon's Grab,"* 187

Clemens Brentano

(Ehrenbreitstein, 1778 – Aschaffenburg, 1842)
Brentano met many of the leading German literary figures while he was still a student. He is best remembered for his work with Arnim on *Des Knaben Wunderhorn* (1805), the first sizable collection of German folk poems.

> Brahms, *"O kühler Wald,"* 146

Achim von Arnim (Berlin, 1781 – Wiepersdorf, 1831)

Arnim studied natural sciences in Halle and Göttingen, where he befriended Clemens Brentano, his partner in compiling *Des Knaben Wunderhorn*. Arnim married Brentano's fiery and creative sister, Bettina. He served as an officer in military actions against Napoleon, 1813–14, and spent his later life on his hereditary estate.

> Mendelssohn, *"Jagdlied,"* 69

Adalbert von Chamisso

(Chateau de Boncourt, Champagne, France, 1781 – Berlin, 1838)
Chamisso grew up in Berlin because his family had been forced to escape from the French Revolution. He is most remembered for a fantastic short novel, *Peter Schlemihl's Remarkable Story*. He was also a significant botanist and philologist.

> R. Schumann, *"Du Ring an meinem Finger,"* 106

Friedrich Rückert (Schweinfurt, 1788 – Berlin, 1866)
Rückert devoted most of his career to Middle Eastern languages, studying, teaching and translating. The personal grief of losing two children led him to write poems that he felt were too private for publication, his *Kindertotenlieder* (Songs on the Death of Children). A surviving daughter published them in 1888, and Gustav Mahler used them in a song cycle for voice and orchestra.

   C. Loewe, *"Süßes Begräbnis,"* 29
   Schubert, *"Lachen und Weinen,"* 49
   R. Schumann, *"Widmung,"* 85
   C. Schumann, *"Liebst du um Schönheit,"* 128

Joseph von Eichendorff
(Ratibor, Upper Silesia, 1788 – Neiße, 1857)
Eichendorff bore the hereditary title of *Freiherr* (free lord). He served as a bureaucrat in the Prussian government, mostly in Berlin and wrote widely read novels that embodied the Romantic spirit. His novels include lyric poems, often loosely connected to the plot. Some of his lyrics, especially about the outdoor life and about the mystique of German forests, were widely sung as popular songs and in settings for male choir by Mendelssohn and others.

   Hensel, *"Nachtwanderer,"* 59
   Mendelssohn, *"Nachtlied,"* 81
   R. Schumann, *"In der Fremde,"* 99

Franz von Schober
(Torup Castle, near Malmö, Sweden, 1796 – Dresden, 1882)
Schober often provided lodging for Schubert, who set seven of his poems to music. Having independent means, Schober never made a settled life. For a few years he was Franz Liszt's secretary.

   Schubert, *"An die Musik,"* 46

Heinrich Heine (Düsseldorf, 1797 – Paris, 1856)
Heine was the first Jewish poet to win respect in Germany. Imitating Wilhelm Müller, the poet of Schubert's *Die Winterreise*, Heine wrote verses that have the stanza form of typical folk songs but are filled with urbane wit and irony. In 1838 he moved to Paris, where he married late in life. Louis Untermeyer made beautiful English translations of Heine's lyrics.

   Mendelssohn, *"Auf Flügeln des Gesanges,"* 75
   R. Schumann, *"Die Lotosblume,"* 96
   R. Schumann, *"Ein Jüngling liebt ein Mädchen,"* 103
   Liszt, *"Du bist wie eine Blume,"* 113
   Franz, *"Aus meinen großen Schmerzen,"* 120

Ludwig Rellstab (Berlin, 1799 – 1860)
Rellstab performed as a child prodigy, playing piano concertos by Mozart. After army service and university study he became a music critic for a major Berlin newspaper. He wrote prolifically in many genres, including novels and verse.

   Schubert, *"Ständchen,"* 53

Georg Friedrich Daumer
(Nuremburg, 1800 – Würzburg, 1875)
Like Goethe and Rückert before him, Daumer studied poetry from Persia and other nations in order to recreate it in German. He lived a quiet and scholarly life.

   Brahms, *"Wir wandelten,"* 160

Nikolaus Lenau
(Csatad, 1802 – Oberdöbling bei Wien, 1850)
Lenau came from a Hungarian noble family, **Niembsch von Strehlenau**, but he is remembered by his pen name. He studied law and medicine, but practiced neither one. In 1832 he bought 400 acres in Ohio, but he did not like America and returned to Germany after a few months. His life ended in an asylum near Vienna.

   Hensel, *"Kommen und Scheiden,"* 64
   Lang, *"An die Entfernte,"* 116

Julius Mosen (Marieney, Vogtland, 1803 – Oldenburg, 1867)
Mosen worked as a lawyer in Dresden while pursuing literature. He aimed to write dramas, but his greatest success was a widely sung ballad about a historical martyr for freedom, Andreas Hofer.

   R. Schumann, *"Der Nussbaum,"* 90

Anton von Zuccalmaglio (1803 – 1869)
Zuccalmaglio was a friend of the Schumanns, but they did not set his poetry to music. In his publications of German folk songs he did not distinguish between older folk material and his own improvements and imitations.

   Brahms, *"Vergebliches Ständchen,"* 150

Eduard Mörike (Ludwigsburg, 1804 – Stuttgart, 1875)
Mörike led an outwardly quiet life as a village pastor and later as a schoolteacher, often limited in his activities by ill health. This contrasts with the rich inner life shown by his poetry, which portrays a great range of human feelings. Mörike married in 1851, but his last years were marred by conflict between his wife and his sister.

   Wolf, *"Der Gärtner,"* 169
   Wolf, *"Fußreise,"* 173
   Wolf, *"Das verlassene Mägdlein,"* 180
   Wolf, *"Gesang Weyla's,"* 184

Hermann von Gilm (Innsbruck, 1812 – Linz, 1864)

Born in the mountainous Tyrol region, Gilm worked in the lower government bureaucracy in several Austrian cities. Several romantic relationships inspired cycles of love poems, but he did not marry until the age of 49.

Strauss, *"Die Nacht,"* 199
Strauss, *"Allerseelen,"* 203

Emanuel Geibel (Lübeck, 1815 – 1884)

Geibel traveled, lived in Athens, and translated Greek poems into German. His original poems (1840), now forgotten, were extremely popular and won him a life long income. He wrote an opera libretto for Mendelssohn, who died too soon to compose it.

Wolf, *"In dem Schatten meiner Locken,"* 191

Wolfgang Müller (Königswinter, 1816 – Neuenahr, 1873)

Müller, having a very common name, called himself Müller von Königswinter after his birthplace. He was a practicing physician, except for a brief political career, until he gave up medicine for literature.

Franz, *"Im Herbst,"* 123

Klaus Groth (Heide, 1819 – Kiel, 1899)

Groth was inspired by Burns's Scottish poems to write poems in his own local dialect, a variety of *Plattdeutsch* (low German). He was a school teacher until by remarkable self-education he won a chair as a university professor.

Brahms, *"Wie Melodien zieht es mir,"* 165

Peter Cornelius (Mainz, 1824 – 1874)

Successful both as a composer and as a poet, Cornelius was a close friend of Paul Heyse and translated works of Hector Berlioz into German. Hugo Wolf admired Cornelius as a poet: "He is one of the truest poets that the Germans have — and fail to appreciate." He was the librettist of his own operas and the poet of most of his own lieder.

Cornelius, *"Ein Ton,"* 133

Paul Heyse (Berlin, 1830 – Munich, 1914)

Having studied Italian folk poetry in Berlin, Heyse took his bride to Italy on a long honeymoon. Supported financially by the King of Bavaria, Heyse lived in Munich. He translated major Italian works into German and wrote original novellas. In 1910, he was the first German to win a Nobel prize for literature.

Wolf, *"Auch kleine Dinge,"* 196

Felix Dahn (Hamburg, 1834 – Breslau, 1912)

Dahn was a professor of law and history and wrote prolifically in those fields. He also wrote, sometimes under the name Ludwig Sophus, plays and other literary works. He also wrote collaborative works with his wife, Therese, a niece of the prominent poet, Annette von Droste-Hülshoff.

Strauss, *"All mein Gedanken, mein Herz*
    und mein Sinn," 208
Strauss, *"Du meines Herzens Krönelein,"* 212

Hans Schmidt (Fellin, 1854–unknown, 1923?)

Schmidt studied at the Leipzig conservatory. He tutored the children of Joseph Joachim, a great violinist and the best friend of Brahms. In 1881 he moved to Vienna and studied musical composition. He later made a career as musician and critic in Riga.

Brahms, *"Sapphische Ode,"* 156

Die Ehre Gottes aus der Natur

[die e̱ːrə gɔtəs ɑos der natuːr]

Nature's Praise of God

die hɪmməl ryːmən dɛs e̱ːvɪgən   e̱ːrə
1. Die Himmel rühmen des Ewigen   Ehre,
The heavens extol   the Eternal-One's honor;

iːr ʃal   pflantst   za̱enən nɑːmən fɔrt
2. Ihr Schall   pflanzt   seinen Namen fort.
their loud-sound communicates his   name   [forwards].

iːn ryːmt der e̱ːrtkraes, iːn pra̱ezən di me̱ːrə
3. Ihn rühmt der Erdkreis,   ihn preisen die Meere;
Him extols the earth-round, him praise   the seas;

fɛrnɪ̱m   o mɛnʃ iːr gœtlɪç vɔrt
4. Vernimm, o Mensch, ihr   göttlich Wort!
hear,   o human, their divine   word!

veːr treːkt der hɪmməl ʊntsɛ̱ːlbɑːrə ʃtɛrnə
5. Wer trägt der Himmel unzählbare   Sterne?
Who carries the heavens' uncountable   stars?

veːr fyːrt di zɔnn aos iːrəm tsɛlt
6. Wer führt die Sonn' aus ihrem Zelt?
Who leads the sun   from its   tent?

ziː kɔmt ʊnt lɔ̱øçtət ʊnt laxt ʊns fɔn fɛ̱rnə
7. Sie kommt und leuchtet und lacht uns von ferne,
It comes and shines and laughs to-us from far-away.

ʊnt lɔøft den veːk glaeç als aen hɛlt
8. Und läuft den Weg, gleich als ein Held.
and runs the way same   as a   hero.

Christian Fürchtegott Gellert (1715–1769)
[krɪsti̯an fy̱rçtəgɔt gɛ̱lərt]

Poetic Background

"May all humankind perceive the greatness of God as Nature shows it." A word for word translation of Gellert's title is "The Honor of God from the Nature." The initial image comes from Psalm 19: "The heavens declare the glory of God; and the firmament sheweth his handywork" (King James Version). Later the psalm says that "the sun. . . rejoiceth as a strong man to run a race."

Beethoven set six of Gellert's odes to music, and even more were composed by Carl Philipp Emmanuel Bach and Johann Adam Hiller. This poem, the most famous of Gellert's odes, consisted of six four-line stanzas; the song uses only the first two. The odd numbered lines have eleven syllables each, the alternating lines, eight.

Line 2: *fortpflanzen* (literally, to plant forth) has several meanings including "to communicate."

Line 3: *Erdkreis* (literally, earth circle) means "the whole round earth."

Line 4: *Vernimm* comes from *vernehmen* (to hear).

Line 6: *Zelt* conveys two images: "dwelling" (in the Bible "tent" is often synonymous with "home") and "canopy." In German poetry the sky is often referred to as a *Zelt*.

Ludwig van Beethoven (1770–1827)
[lu̱ːtvɪç van be̱ːthoːfən]

Musical Background

Beethoven's non-creedal religion was based in Nature and in ethics. His Gellert songs were not written for liturgical worship services, but for amateur singers at home. They were a memorial to Countess Anna Margarete von Browne, who with her husband had been Beethoven's strong financial supporter. She died unexpectedly on May 15, 1803; these songs were published about three months later.

The style indication is *Majestätisch und erhaben* (majestic and solemn, or sublime). The time signature is *alla breve*, two beats to a measure, and the tempo must not drag. The song demands long phrases; if possible, the first line of verse should be sung with a single breath.

Like most lieder composers, Beethoven expected singers to follow the dynamics in the piano part. Both performers must understand that *fortissimo* means "very strong." If they take it to mean "as loud as possible," the result will be too harsh. As the voice enters, the dynamic drops to the same *forte* level as will be used for the second phrase, *"Ihr Schall. . ."* The piano must be subordinate to the voice, especially when doubling the same notes. As always in Classical style, use of the pedal should be minimal, but pedal use may be implied by the *portato* articulation from m19 and at least through m26.

This song is not long, but Beethoven filled it with grandeur and with surprises. Just after a wide leap in m4, a diminuendo leads to an awesome hush on the word *Ehre*. Modulations beginning in m11 depict the way the poet admires the earth, sea and starry sky in turn. As the tonic key returns in m29, the sun rises and fills the sky with God's light.

The power of Beethoven's music has made this a concert favorite in arrangements for mixed or male choruses.

Sources

Text: *Geistliche Oden und Lieder*, 1757. This version: *Gellert's Dichtungen*. Leipzig: Bibliographisches Institut, 1891.
Music, autograph lost. First edition: *Sechs Lieder von Gellert*, Opus 48, No. 4. Vienna: Artaria, August, 1803. Dedication to Count von Browne. Original key: C.

Die Ehre Gottes aus der Natur

C. F. Gellert

Ludwig van Beethoven
(Range: C4 – G5)

Majestätisch und erhaben ⓐ

Die Him - mel rüh - men des E - wi - gen Eh - re, ihr

Schall pflanzt sei - nen Na - men___ fort. Ihn rühmt der Erd - kreis, ihn

prei - sen die Mee - re; ver - nimm, o Mensch, ihr gött - lich Wort!

ⓐ "Majestic and solemn." *Majestätisch,* or in Italian *maestoso,* is a tempo between *moderato* and *allegro,* according to Muzio Clementi, *Introduction to the Art of Playing on the Pianoforte* (London: Clementi et al., 1801, p. 13; reprint by Da Capo Press, 1974). Suggestion: ♩ = ca. 66 M.M.

ⓑ The three grace notes are played quickly, beginning on the downbeat, that is, simultaneously with the lower notes of the chord (Clementi, *op. cit.,* page 10).

Translation: The heavens extol God's honor; their sound communicates his name. The whole earth extols him and the seas praise him; hear, o mankind, their divine word!

Wer trägt der Him-mel un-zähl-ba-re Ster-ne?

Wer führt die Sonn' aus ih - rem Zelt? Sie

kommt und leuch-tet und lacht uns von fer - ne, und läuft den Weg, gleich als ein

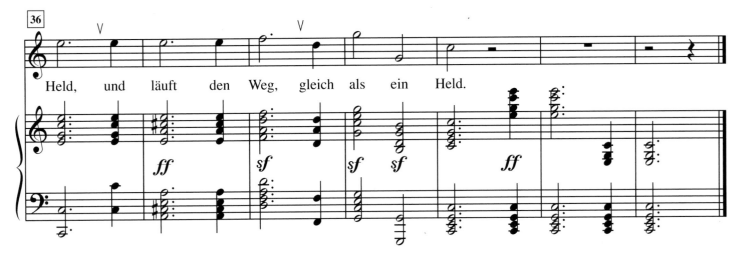

Held, und läuft den Weg, gleich als ein Held.

Who holds up the uncountable stars of the heavens? Who leads the sun forth from its dwelling? It comes and shines and beams on us from afar and runs its course like a champion.

Sehnsucht
Longing

Ludwig van Beethoven (1770–1827)

nuːr weːr   diː zeːnzʊxt   kɛnt
1. **Nur wer   die Sehnsucht kennt,**
Only one-who (-) longing   knows

vaes vas ɪç laedə
2. **Weiß, was ich leide!**
knows what I   suffer!

allaen ʊnt ʔapgətrɛnt
3. **Allein und abgetrennt**
Alone and separated

fɔn alːlər frɔødə
4. **Von aller Freude,**
from all   joy

zeː ɪç ans fɪrmamɛnt
5. **Seh' ich ans   Firmament**
look I   at-the firmament

nax   jeːnər zaetə
6. **Nach jener Seite.**
toward that   side.

ax deːr   mɪç liːpt ʊnt kɛnt
7. **Ach! der   mich liebt und kennt,**
Ah, he-who my   loves and knows

ɪst ɪn der vaetə
8. **Ist in der Weite.**
is in the distance.

ɛs ʃvɪndəlt   miːr ɛs brɛnt
9. **Es schwindelt mir, es brennt**
it dizzies   me, it burns

maen aengəvaedə
10. **Mein Eingeweide.**
my   inner-parts.

11. **Nur wer die Sehnsucht kennt,**

12. **Weiß, was ich leide!**

Johann Wolfgang von Goethe
[joːhan vɔlfgaŋ fɔn gøːtə]
(1749 – 1832)

Poetic Background

"I am alone here, understood by no one." The character portrayed in these words is a mysterious waif named Mignon, a character in a novel, *Wilhelm Meister's Lehrjahre* (learning years, or apprenticeship).

In the German craft system an apprentice is called a *Lehrling* and a master craftsman is a *Meister*. In the novel an apprentice in the art of life becomes a master through years of life experience.

Unhappy in love, young Wilhelm joins a wandering troupe of actors in hope of becoming a competent actor. On his travels he meets fascinating people, among them Mignon, a child of 12 or 13. She is a talented but unwilling performer in a troupe of child acrobats. She usually wears trousers, and at first encounter Wilhelm is unsure whether she is a boy or girl. When Wilhelm rescues Mignon from a public beating by the manager of the acrobatic troupe, she willingly accepts his protection. Because she is so young, Wilhelm fails to notice that she falls in love with him.

By chance Wilhelm also meets an elderly blind man who plays the harp and sings. One day while Wilhelm is resting in his room in a mood of lovesickness, he overhears Mignon and the Harper singing this melancholy song outside his window. (In Goethe's novel both the Harper and Mignon sing from time to time, presumably in Italian as they both speak only broken German.)

Goethe enclosed this poem in June 1785 with a letter to Charlotte von Stein. She was far away in Karlsbad, and he was "longing" for her to return to Weimar. The poem consists of one 12-line stanza. The odd-numbered lines all rhyme with *kennt*, and the alternating lines more or less rhyme with *leide* (*Freude* is accepted as an inexact rhyme). Lines 11–12 are identical with lines 1–2.

The title is Beethoven's; the poem has no title in the novel.

Line 1: *kennt* (is familiar with) contrasts with *weiß* (knows as a fact) in line 2. German uses different words for these two ways of knowing.

Line 5: *Firmament* (sky) has the connotation of a broad expanse of starry sky.

Line 6: *jener Seite* means "far side" (of the mountains), referring to the longing of both Mignon and the Harper for their homeland, Italy.

Line 7: *der mich liebt* is not identified. Not knowing the Harper's true identity, Mignon might be thinking of her father, but the line is not very appropriate for the Harper to sing.

Line 9: *Es* is the impersonal subject of the verb *schwindelt* (is-dizzy); *mir* (to-me) clarifies who is affected by the dizziness. The second *es* fills the place of the subject so that the real subject can be placed after the verb *brennt*.

Line 10: *Eingeweide* (intestines) stands here for all of one's inner self. The image of the inner organs burning also occurs in Luther's translation of the Psalms into German.

Musical Background

Beethoven composed four settings of Mignon's song in 1807 and early 1808. He wrote a note on the front side of the manuscript: "I did not have enough time to produce a good song, so four attempts." The first three settings are unsatisfying because they use the same music for the second half of the poem as for the first half, providing no sense of emotional climax.

Beethoven's fourth "attempt" produced a wonderful miniature, fully worthy of the poem. Mignon's melody begins simply and beautifully in an Italian style. To highlight the word *abgetrennt* the melody repeatedly hesitates, but it gathers energy as Mignon looks to the sky. The music moves to a major key with the thought that someone knows and loves her. It seems that she sings the words *in der Weite* without realizing what they mean, but then she feels a physical reaction in her body as the music plunges suddenly back to minor. She regains her composure to sing her opening melody again. As she repeats line 2 of her song (Beethoven added the word *ja* [jaː]), the word *was* dips to a flatted tone, a perfect example of the pathos of the Neapolitan tone and its associated harmony.

Beethoven was not alone in making "attempts" at this

song. Goethe's friend, Karl Friedrich Zelter, wrote three settings of Mignon's song. Schubert wrote six settings, including choral settings and a duet for soprano and tenor. Mignon's and the Harper's songs were also set to music by Loewe, Schumann and Wolf, among the dozens of other composers. The most famous setting of all was Tchaikovsky's 1869 song, known in English as "None but the lonely heart," Opus 6, No. 6.

Sources

Text: *Wilhelm Meister's Lehrjahre*, Book 4, Chapter 11. 1795. This version: Goethe. *Werke*, vol 3, pp. 670–671. Berlin: Tempel Verlag, 1959.

Music: autograph, dated March 3, 1808, is in the Bodmer collection, Zürich. First edition: *"Sehnsucht" in vier Kompositionen* [WoO (Work without opus number) 134]. Vienna and Pest: Kunst und Industrie Comptoir, early 1810. Original key: G minor.

Sehnsucht

J. W. von Goethe

Ludwig van Beethoven
(Range: G♯4 – F5)

(a) "Very slow." Adagio is the slowest of all tempo markings, according to Muzio Clementi, *Introduction to the Art of Playing on the Pianoforte* (London: Clementi et al., 1801, page 13; reprint by Da Capo Press, 1974.). Suggestion: ♪ = ca. 84

Translation: Only one who has felt longing knows what I suffer. Alone and isolated from all joy, I gaze at the sky to the south.

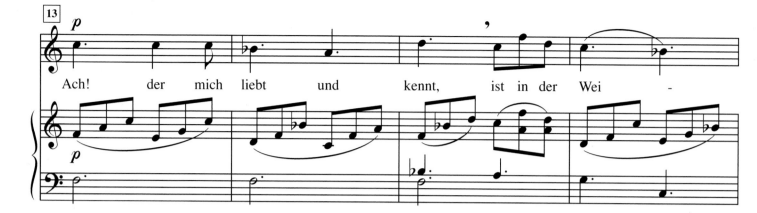

Ah, the one who knows and loves me is far away. I feel dizzy, my inner organs are on fire.

Aus Goethe's Faust
[aos gøːtəs faost]
From Goethe's *Faust*

Ludwig van Beethoven (1770–1827)

ɛs vaːr aenmaːl aen køːnɪç
1. Es war einmal ein König,
There was once a king

der hat aenən groːsən floː
2. Der hatt' einen großen Floh,
who had a big flea;

den liːpt er gaːr nɪçt veːnɪç
3. Den lieb' er gar nicht wenig,
him loved he at-all not little,

als viː zaenən aegnən zoːn
4. Als wie seinen eignen Sohn.
as like his own son.

daː riːf eːr zaenən ʃnaedər
5. Da rief er seinen Schneider,
Then called he his tailor,

der ʃnaedər kaːm heraːn
6. Der Schneider kam heran:
the tailor came before-him:

daː mɪs dem jʊŋkər klaedər
7. "Da, miß dem Junker Kleider
"Here, measure for-the young-sir clothes

ʊnt mɪs iːm hoːzən aːn
8. Und miß ihm Hosen an!"
and measure for-him trousers [-]."

ɪn zamːət ʊnt ɪn zaedə
9. In Sammet und in Seide
In velvet and in silk

vaːr eːr nuːn aːngətaːn
10. War er nun angetan,
was he now dressed,

hatə bɛndər aof dem klaedə
11. Hatte Bänder auf dem Kleide,
had ribbons on the clothing

hat aox aen krɔøts daraːn
12. Hatt auch ein Kreuz daran,
had also a cross thereupon,

ʊnt vaːr zoglaeç minɪstər
13. Und war sogleich Minister,
and was immediately minister

ʊnt hat aenən groːsən ʃtɛrn
14. Und hatt einen großen Stern.
and had a big star.

daː vʊrdən zaenə gəʃvɪstər
15. Da wurden seine Geschwister
Then became his siblings

bae hoːf aox groːsə hɛrn
16. Bei Hof auch große Herrn.
at court also great personages.

ʊnt hɛrn ʊnt fraon am hoːfə
17. Und Herrn und Frau'n am Hofe,
And gentlemen and ladies at court,

diː vaːrən zeːr gəplaːkt
18. Die waren sehr geplagt,
they were very tormented,

diː køːnɪgɪn ʊnt diː tsoːfə
19. Die Königin und die Zofe
the queen and the chambermaid

gəʃtɔxən ʊnt gənaːkt
20. Gestochen und genagt,
bitten and gnawed,

ʊnt dʊrftən ziː nɪçt knɪkən
21. Und durften sie nicht knicken
and were-allowed they not to-snap

ʊnt vɛk ziː jukən nɪçt
22. Und weg sie jucken nicht.
and away them scratch not.

viːr knɪkən ʊnt ɛrʃtɪkən
23. Wir knicken und ersticken
We snap and suffocate

dɔx glaeç vɛn aenər ʃtɪçt
24. Doch gleich, wenn einer sticht.
Indeed right-away when one bites.

Johann Wolfgang von Goethe
(1749–1832)

Poetic Background

"Let me tell you how foolishly people behave when they have too much power." The singer is Mephistopheles, a devil who has made himself visible in order to deal with Dr. Johannes Faust.

Fantastic tales were told about the magic powers of the real Dr. Faust, who died in 1540. In 1587 an anonymous book told of a minor demon named Mephistopheles, who gave Faust his evil powers and who claimed his soul for Hell in the hereafter. The sensational story was taken to England, where Christopher Marlowe used it for his greatest play, *Tragical History of Doctor Faustus* (1604). In Marlowe's final scene Faustus realizes that he has given up eternity in Heaven in return for a few years of meaningless earthly powers.

In childhood Goethe saw Faust plays done with puppets and filled with magic tricks and crude humor. In a dramatic sketch that he wrote at the age of 25, he completely transformed the raw material of the story. Goethe replaced the trivial humor of the folk plays with a devil who looks on everything human with a cynical attitude.

Old Faust, disillusioned with life and unable to take the thought of Heaven seriously, promises his soul to Mephistopheles in return for another chance at youth. After they strike a bargain and Faust is transformed into a young man, Mephistopheles takes him to Auerbach's Tavern, where students from the University of Leipzig are carousing. Faust is shy in his new role, but Mephistopheles is the life of the party. To entertain the students he sings this cynical song about a foolish king.

The song establishes Mephistopheles' character as one that scorns conventional authority but on a light-hearted, superficial level. At this early point in the play the tragic results of Faust's bargain with the devil are still unforeseen.

Line 10: in *angetan* the first syllable had a long vowel in Goethe's time but not in modern German.

Lines 11, 12: *Bänder* and *Kreuz* are decorations such as a military officer wears.

Line 15: *Geschwister* includes both male and female siblings.

Musical Background

The piano introduction depicts the jumping flea in the treble and Mephistopheles' deriding laughter in the bass. The voice begins a solemn narration, which continues in a straightforward manner until the whole story has been told. At that point a chorus of students breaks in (m70), just as Goethe indicated in the play. (In reality, a soloist can finish the song quite effectively without help from a chorus.)

To write a truly comic song is not easy; very few composers have tried to match Beethoven's success with this poem. The best of all, however, is Mussorgsky's Russian version, known in English as "The Song of the Flea."

In the corresponding scene of Gounod's opera *Faust* Méphisto sings an aria, *"Le veau d'or"* (the calf of gold), about the power of money. The effect is cynical, but not humorous.

In the postlude Beethoven suggested a comical fingering: pairs of 32nd notes all played with the thumb. The pianist is supposed to play them by rocking the side of the thumb over two keys as if in the act of squashing insects.

Sources

Text, first version: *Faust* [now known as *Urfaust* (original Faust)]. 1774, published in 1887. This song occurs in the scene *"Auerbachs Keller."* First edition: *Faust, ein Fragment,* 1790, also *Faust, der Tragödie erster Teil,* (Part I) 1808. This version: *Werke,* vol. 2. Berlin: Tempel Verlag, 1959.

Music, autograph lost. (Sketches for this song predate 1800.) First edition: *Sechs Gesänge,* Opus 75, No. 4. Leipzig: Breitkopf und Härtel, 1810. Also this song alone as a supplement to the *Allgemeine musikalische Zeitung,* October 3, 1810. Original key: G minor.

Aus Goethe's Faust

J. W. von Goethe

Ludwig van Beethoven
(Range: D4 – E5)

Es war ein-mal ein Kö-nig,   der hatt' ei-nen gro-ßen Floh,   den liebt' er gar nicht

we-nig,   als   wie sei-nen eig-nen_ Sohn.   Da_ rief er sei-nen Schnei-der, der

ⓐ Suggestion: ♩ = ca. 72 M.M.

Translation: Once upon a time there was a king who had a big flea. He loved it greatly, as if it were his own son. He called his tailor, and

Schnei-der kam her - an: "Da, miss dem Jun - ker Klei - der und miss ihm Ho - sen—

an!"

In Sam-met und in Sei - de war er nun— an - ge - tan, hat - te Bän-der auf dem

ⓑ Sing *"kam"* on two equal 16th notes.

ⓒ The irregular beaming is Beethoven's.

ⓓ In this song all grace notes in the piano part are played quickly, on the beat.

when the tailor came, said: "Measure the young fellow for a coat and trousers!" In velvet and silk he was now dressed and wore official decorations

Klei - de,   hatt' auch ein_ Kreuz da - ran,   und_ war so - gleich Mi -

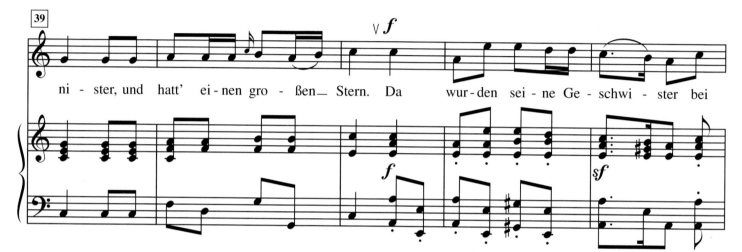

ni - ster, und hatt' ei - nen gro - ßen_ Stern. Da   wur - den sei - ne Ge - schwi - ster bei

Hof auch gro - ße_   Herrn.

and even a cross. He was promoted to government minister and wore a big star. All of his siblings also became great figures at court.

e "*Chor*" indicates that a unison chorus takes over. Beethoven was imagining the scene as it takes place in *Faust*. A chorus is not required.

And the ladies and gentlemen of the court were tormented, the queen and her chambermaid were bitten and gnawed.
And they weren't allowed to crack them or even brush them away. But we can squash and smother them right away
when they bite.

(f) Beethoven used separate flags rather than beams for these notes.

(g) In the original key (G) the notes played by the right hand in mm. 80–81 are all white keys. Beethoven fingered them "1–1" meaning that the thumb plays each pair of notes with a rocking motion as if squashing insects. In this key Beethoven's instruction can be followed only on the notes B-A.

Mädchen sind wie der Wind
Young Girls Are Like the Wind

Carl Loewe (1796–1869)
[karl løːvə]

mɛːtçən zɪnt viː der vɪnt
1. **Mädchen sind wie der Wind,**
Girls   are   like the wind:

ʃɛŋkən ɔft ɪm ʃɛrtsə
2. **Schenken oft   im Scherze,**
they-give often in play,

hɔøtə miːr mɔrgən diːr
3. **Heute mir,   morgen dir,**
today to-me, tomorrow to-you,

flatərhaft iːr hɛrtsə
4. **Flatterhaft ihr Herze.**
fickly   their hearts.

trɑoə nɪçt diːzə ʃprɪçt
5. **Traue nicht! Diese   spricht:**
Trust not!   This-one says:

liːpçən diːr tsu diːnən
6. **"Liebchen, dir zu dienen!"**
"Darling,   you to   serve!"

ʃmaeçəlae hɔøçəlae
7. **Schmeichelei, Heuchelei**
Flattery,   hypocrisy,

laxt ɑos iːrən miːnən
8. **Lacht aus ihren Mienen.**
laughs from their facial-expressions.

voː ziː geːn voː zeː ʃteːn
9. **Wo   sie gehn, wo   sie stehn,**
Wherever they go,   wherever they stay,

vɛn ziː dɪç ɑox kʏsən
10. **Wenn sie dich auch küssen,**
even-if they thee also kiss,

veːrdən ziː dɔrt ʊnt hiː
11. **Werden sie dort und hie,**
will   they there and here

vas tsuː tɑːdəln vɪsən
12. **Was   zu tadeln wissen.**
something to criticize know.

ʃøːn ʊnt rʊnt lɔkt iːr mʊnt
13. **Schön und rund lockt   ihr Mund**
Pretty and round entices her mouth

tsvɑːr mɪt zyːsem ʃallə
14. **Zwar mit süßem Schalle.**
indeed with sweet   sound.

ʃlɑo fɛrdɛkt ɑːbər ʃtɛkt
15. **Schlau verdeckt aber   steckt**
cleverly hidden,   however, is

dɔx ɪm hɛrtsən gallə
16. **Doch im   Herzen Galle.**
indeed in-the heart   gall.

Anonymous

Poetic Background

"Girls are a lot of fun, but don't trust them with your heart!" Any young man is likely to have felt this way, at least sometimes.

When Loewe wrote this song as a young man of 22, he was near the end of his studies at the University of Halle. It is not known how he obtained the text, but it had been used earlier by other composers. The earliest of them, Johann André (1741–1799), said that the author of the text was "W."

Musical Background

Real musical humor is a rare commodity. Aside from the humorous words, here even the music could make us laugh. It starts like no other song: a scale in octaves rushes to the downbeat as quickly as the pianist can play it. After four quick measures in 3/8 the meter changes to 3/4, but soon cross accents occur that leave the listener just as confused about the meter as the young man is about girls.

What Loewe wrote here in 1818 is rare in any music written between 1700 and 1900. The eighth notes, which are constant through all of the meters used, are grouped either in pairs (in 3/4) or in threes (in 3/8), which are even mixed unpredictably (in 7/8). The rhythmic scheme is "additive," that is, small values are added together to make a variety of measure lengths. This contrasts with the Classical norm, "divisive" rhythms, in which measures of uniform length are divided into notes of various lengths. Additive rhythms had occurred in earlier music until the early Baroque, but not again until Stravinsky reintroduced them in the early 1900s.

Loewe's 7/8 meter can be understood as 2/4 + 3/8. Even later Romantic composers who used unusual meters, such as Brahms and Mussorgsky, did not alternate them so quickly with other meters. The fast tempo adds to an effect of giddiness.

Loewe added even more surprises: each of the four stanzas begins with a completely different melody in the voice part, although the piano part is nearly identical each time. As a whole, the song guarantees fun for both performers and audiences.

Sources

Text: The poem has not been published apart from music.
Music: *Heitere Gesänge* (Cheerful Songs), Opus 9, Book 6, No. 4. Leipzig: Hofmeister, 1828. Original key: G.

Mädchen sind wie der Wind

Anonymous

Carl Loewe
(Range: A3 or C♯4 – F♯5)

ⓐ "Quickly." Suggestion: ♪ = ca. 208

Translation: Girls are changeable as the wind; they are apt to give their hearts playfully— today to me, tomorrow to you. Don't be trusting! One says, " Darling, anything for you!" Flattery, insincerity laughs in her mouth.

Wherever they are, whether here or there, even if they kiss you, they will find fault with something about you. Pretty mouths, round and tempting, even with pretty voices,

Schlau ver-deckt   a - ber steckt   doch im Her-zen Gal - le.

Mäd - chen— sind   wie der Wind,

schen-ken   oft   im Scher-ze,   heu-te mir, mor-gen dir,

flat-ter-haft ihr Her - ze.   Mäd-chen sind   wie der Wind.

but cleverly hidden in their hearts— poison!

Süßes Begräbnis

[zy:səs bəgrɛ:pnɪs]
Sweet Burial

Carl Loewe (1796–1869)

ʃɛ:fərɪn	ax	vi:	hɑ:bən
1. Schäferin,	**ach,**	**wie**	**haben**
Shepherdess,	ah,	how	have

zi:	dɪç	zo:	zy:s	bəgrɑ:bən
2. Sie	**dich**	**so**	**süß**	**begraben!**
they	you	so	sweetly	buried!

a:lə	lʏftə	hɑ:bən	gəʃtø:nət
3. Alle	**Lüfte**	**haben**	**gestöhnet,**
All	breezes	have	moaned,

maeənglɔkən	tsu:	grɑ:p	di:r	gətø:nət
4. Maienglocken	**zu**	**Grab**	**dir**	**getönet.**
may-bells	at	grave	to-you	rang.

gly:vʊrm	vɔltə	di:	fakəl	trɑ:gən
5. Glühwurm	**wollte**	**die**	**Fackel**	**tragen,**
Glowworm	wanted	the	torch	to-carry,

ʃtɛrn	i:m	zɛlpst	ɛs	tɛ:t	vɛrzɑ:gən
6. Stern	**ihm**	**selbst**	**es**	**tät**	**versagen.**
star	him	self	it	did	deny.

naxt	gɪŋ	ʃvarts	ɪn	trɑoərflø:rən
7. Nacht	**ging**	**schwarz**	**in**	**Trauerflören,**
Night	went	black		in mourning-ribbons,

ʊnt	al	i:rə	ʃatən	gɪŋən	ɪn	kø:rən
8. Und	**all'**	**ihre**	**Schatten**	**gingen**	**in**	**Chören.**
and	all	its	shadows	walked	in	choruses.

di:	trɛ:nən	vɪrt	di:r	das mɔrgənro:t	vaenən
9. Die	**Tränen**	**wird**	**dir**	**das Morgenrot**	**weinen,**
The tears	will	for-you	the morning-red	weep,

ʊnt den ze:gən	di: zɔn	ɑofs	grɑ:p	di:r	ʃaenən
10. Und den Segen	**die Sonn'**	**auf's**	**Grab**	**dir**	**scheinen.**
and the blessing	the sun	on-the	grave	to-you	shine.

11. Schäferin, ach, wie haben

12. Sie dich so süß begraben!

Friedrich Rückert (1788–1866)
[fri:drɪç rʏkərt]

Poetic Background

"A sweet creature has died, and the beautiful things of Nature have come together to beautify her burial." This is sung with great love for the departed shepherdess and calm satisfaction that her sweet nature is honored by the beauty that surrounds her resting place.

In earlier literature there was a tradition of pastoral poetry, consisting of lyrics and plays about the supposedly simple, happy lives of shepherds and shepherdesses. Rückert, who wrote some of the tenderest and most musical sounding lyric poems of his time, placed this poem within that tradition by addressing it to a departed shepherdess.

One cannot be sure, however, that this poem is merely a pastoral fantasy. It may have been written after a painful tragedy, the deaths of a daughter Luise on December 31, 1833, and a son Ernst three weeks later, both victims of scarlet fever. Rückert did not date his published poems, but it seems possible that he addressed this poem to his deceased four-year-old daughter and concealed his deep personal grief by addressing her as if she were a fairy-tale "shepherdess."

Rückert arranged the poem in three unequal stanzas: lines 1–2, 3–10 and 11–12.

Lines 1 and 11: *ach*, in Loewe's song, *o* in Rückert's poem.

Musical Background

Loewe felt a kinship with Rückert and set more than 30 of his poems to music. By the time Loewe composed this song in October, 1837, he was famous throughout northern Germany. He had published more than a hundred songs. His baritone voice was much admired, and eventually he went on a number of international tours as a singer of his own songs.

This serene and lovely song requires a legato line of the utmost sensitivity. A steady tempo is advisable nearly throughout, with broadening for the climax at . . .*und den Segen die Sonn'*. . . There is an inspired moment at the words *so süß*, as the piano stops doubling the voice part and instead leaps to its own melody a third higher, finishing the song with the illusion of a vocal duet.

Sources

Text, first publication: *Gedichte*. Erlangen, 1834–38. This version: *Rückerts Werke*, vol. 3. Berlin: Bong, n.d.

Music: *Rückerts Gedichte*, Opus 62, No. 4. Berlin: Westphal, 1838. Original key: B.

Süßes Begräbnis

Friedrich Rückert

Carl Loewe
(Range: B3 – E5)

ⓐ Suggestion: ♪ = ca. 86

Translation: Shepherdess, how sweetly they have buried you!

The breezes moaned and maybells rang you to your grave. The glowworm wanted to provide your torch, but a star took over the duty.

Night was robed in mourning, and its shadows walked in procession. The morning dawn will shed tears for you, and the sun will

Grab— dir— schei - nen.

Schä - fe - rin, ach,— wie ha - ben sie dich so süß————— be -

gra - ben!

sempre più piano

shine a blessing on your grave.

Das Rosenband, D. 280
[das ro̲ːzənbant]
The Ribbon of Roses

Franz Schubert (1797–1828)
[frants ʃuːbərt]

ɪm fry̲ːlɪŋsʃatən fant ɪç ziː
1. Im Frühlingsschatten fand ich sie;
In-the spring-shade   found I   her;

daː bant ɪç ziː mɪt ro̲ːzənbɛndərn
2. Da band ich sie mit Rosenbändern:
then bound I   her with rose-ribbons.

ziː fyːlt ɛs nɪçt ʊnt ʃlu̲mːərtə
3. Sie fühlt' es nicht, und schlummerte.
She felt   it not   and slept.

ɪç zaː   ziː aːn maen le̲ːbən hɪŋ
4. Ich sah   sie an; mein Leben hing
I   looked-at her [-]; my life   hung

mɪt ‿ di̲ːzəm blɪk   aːn i̲ːrəm le̲ːbən
5. Mit diesem Blick an ihrem Leben:
with this   glance on her   life.

ɪç fyːlt ɛs voːl ʊnt vʊst ɛs nɪçt
6. Ich fühlt' es wohl, und wußt' es nicht.
I   felt   it indeed and knew it not.

dɔx lɪspəlt ɪç iːr ʃpra̲ːxloːs tsuː
7. Doch lispelt' ich ihr sprachlos zu,
But whispered I   to-her speechlessly [-]

ʊnt ra̲ʊʃtə mɪt den ro̲ːzənbɛndərn
8. Und rauschte mit den Rosenbändern:
and rustled with the rose-ribbons;

daː va̲xtə ziː fɔm ʃlu̲mːər ʔaʊf
9. Da wachte sie vom Schlummer auf.
then woke   she from slumber   up.

ziː zaː   mɪç aːn iːr le̲ːbən hɪŋ
10. Sie sah   mich an; ihr Leben hing
She looked at-me [-]; her life   hung

mɪt ‿ di̲ːzəm blɪk   aːn ma̲enəm le̲ːbən
11. Mit diesem Blick an meinem Leben,
with this   glance on my   life,

ʊnt ʊm   ʊns varts   ely̲ːziʊm
12. Und um   uns ward's Elysium.
and around us became-it Elysium.

Friedrich Gottlieb Klopstock (1724 – 1803)
[fri̲ːdrɪç gɔtliːp klɔp.ʃtɔk]

Poetic Background

"On the happiest day of my life it was as if my beloved and I were in Heaven."

Klopstock is writing about the love of his own life, Margarethe Moller, whom he called Meta and, in poems, Cidli. This poem dates from 1753, the year before he married her.

The poem is in four stanzas of three lines each. Klopstock seldom used rhyme, which was felt to be "modern." For Schubert's generation this poem was an admired classic.

Line 1: *Frühlingsschatten* is a famous example of a poetic compound word; it has an evocative quality without drawing any rational connection between springtime and shadows. Instead of this word Schubert used *Frühlingsgarten* (spring's garden), a somewhat less imaginative word. Klopstock capitalized the pronoun *sie* as *Sie*, an unusual sign of respect for the beloved.

Line 2: *band* cannot be taken too literally since roses are thorny. He means that he surrounded her with roses, probably to enjoy the sight, but also so that she would smell them.

Line 4: *hing,* in the sense of "depended." "My whole life depended on what she might say or do." Luckily, his love is reciprocated (line 10).

Line 7: *lispelt'* in modern German means "lisped," but in poetry "whispered." *Sprachlos* here signifies "without words."

Line 12: *ward's*; Schubert omitted the *'s. Elysium* was, in Greek mythology, a place of ideal happiness for the blessed dead; also known as "Elysian Fields."

Musical Background

In September 1815, when Schubert wrote this song, he was 18 and teaching in his father's school. He disliked teaching and used all of his spare time to compose. He was still taking composition lessons with Antonio Salieri.

Schubert invariably used Italian tempo indications for his instrumental music but German indications for his lieder. *Mäßig, lieblich* means "moderate, lovely." The meter is in two beats to a measure and tempo is not slow.

The voice part is organized in two identical stanzas. What is surprising is the delicacy and smoothness with which the piano part is turned into a variation for the second stanza. Schubert composed three "Cidli" songs, all in A♭.

After Schubert's death Anton Diabelli undertook to issue all of his unpublished songs in a series of small volumes. The series is referred to as the *Nachlass* (estate, left behind when one dies). Diabelli sometimes added piano introductions to songs that had none, and his introduction to *"Das Rosenband"* still appears in some editions.

A number of other composers have set Klopstock's *"Das Rosenband"* to music, including an elaborate version by Richard Strauss. None of them rivals Schubert's song for sincerity and warmth.

Sources

Text: *Klopstock's sämmtliche Werke,* Vol. 1, *Oden.* Leipzig: G. J. Göschen, 1823.

Music: The autograph is lost. First edition: *Gedichte von Klopstock.* Wien: A. Diabelli, 1837. Original key: A♭.

Das Rosenband, D. 280

F. G. Klopstock

Franz Schubert
(Range: F3 – F4)

(a) "Moderately, lovely." Suggestion: ♩ = ca. 52.

(b) Sing the appoggiatura as a quarter note, completely replacing the note of resolution.

Translation: In the spring I found her sleeping in the shade; I tied her with ribbons of rosebuds. She felt nothing and went on sleeping. I gazed at her. With this gaze, I felt that my life depended on her life. Indeed I felt it, unconsciously. But I whispered wordlessly to her and

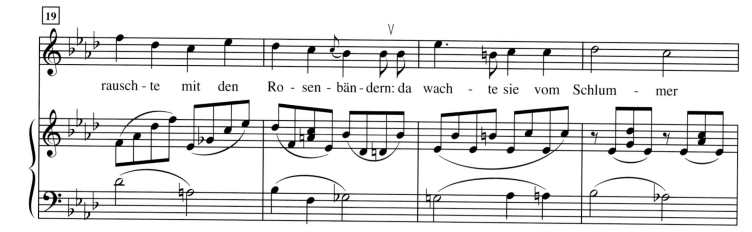

19

rausch - te mit den Ro - sen - bän - dern: da wach - te sie vom Schlum - mer

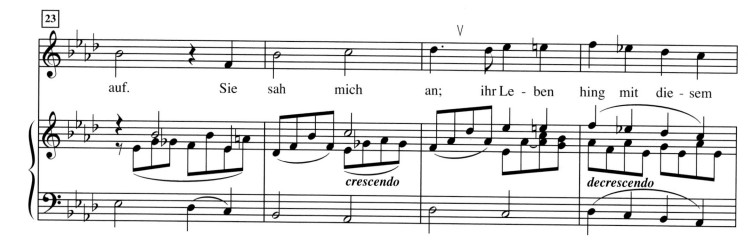

23

auf. Sie sah mich an; ihr Le - ben hing mit die - sem

crescendo　　　*decrescendo*

27

Blick an mei - nem Le - ben, und um uns ward's E -

crescendo

31

ly - si - um.

p

rustled the ribbons of rosebuds. Then she awoke from sleep. She gazed at me. With this gaze, her life depended on my life, and all around us it was like the Elysian Fields.

Seligkeit, D. 433

[zeːlɪçkaet]
Blessedness

Franz Schubert (1797–1828)

froødən zɔndər tsɑːl
1. **Freuden sonder Zahl**
Joys   beyond number

blyːn ɪm hɪmməls.zɑːl
2. **Blüh'n im Himmelssaal!**
bloom in heaven's-big-room,

ɛŋəln ʊnt fɛrklɛːrtən
3. **Engeln und Verklärten,**
Angels and transfigured-persons,

viː diː fɛːtər leːrtən
4. **Wie die Väter lehrten.**
as the fathers taught.

oː dɑː mœçt ɪç zaen
5. **O da möcht' ich sein**
Oh, there would I be

ʊnt mɪç eːvɪç froøn
6. **Und mich ewig freun!**
and myself eternally enjoy!

jeːdəm lɛçəlt traot
7. **Jedem lächelt traut**
To-each-man smiles fondly

aenə hɪmməlsbraot
8. **Eine Himmelsbraut;**
a heaven's-bride,

harf ʊnt psaltər klɪŋət
9. **Harf' und Psalter klinget,**
harp and psaltery sound,

ʊnt man tantst ʊnt zɪŋət
10. **Und man tanzt und singet.**
and one dances and sings.

11. **O da möcht' ich sein,**

12. **Und mich ewig freun!**

liːbər blaeb ʔɪç hiːr
13. **Lieber bleib' ich hier,**
Rather stay I here

lɛçəlt laura miːr
14. **Lächelt Laura mir**
if-smiles Laura to-me

aenən blɪk der zɑːgət
15. **Einen Blick, der saget,**
a glance that says

das ɪç ɑosgəklɑːgət
16. **Dass ich ausgeklaget.**
that I have-finished-mourning.

zeːlɪç dan mɪt iːr
17. **Selig dann mit ihr,**
Blessed then with her,

blaeb ɪç eːvɪç hiːr
18. **Bleib' ich ewig hier!**
am-staying I eternally here!

Ludwig Heinrich Christoph Hölty
[luːtvɪç haenrɪç krɪstɔf hœlti]
(1748 – 1776)

Poetic Background

"Heaven must be beautiful, but as long as Laura loves me I prefer this life."

Hölty called this poem *"Minnelied"* (Love Song), using an ancient word for love. The medieval Minnesingers, who lived in the 1100–1300s, wrote songs in praise of women whom they admired from afar. The name Laura also has medieval associations: a young woman named Laura was adored from a distance by the Italian poet Petrarch (1304–1374). Ever since then, Laura has been a name by which poets can address their ladies when it would be indiscreet to publish their real names.

Hölty wrote this poem on February 13, 1773. He was in love with Anna Juliane Hagemann, who remained his "Laura," his unattainable ideal.

Line 3: *Verklärten* are persons whose bodies have been transformed into radiant beings in Heaven.

Line 4: *Väter* may be understood either as ancestors or as the "Church Fathers," the earliest writers about the Christian faith after the writing of the New Testament.

Line 9: *Psalter* is an ancient plucked stringed instrument.

Musical Background

When he wrote this song in May 1816, Schubert and his friends were planning how to approach publishing his first songs. None of them had been performed in public, but they were heard at musical evenings at the homes of Schubert's friends. These parties came to be called "Schubertiades."

Some of Schubert's songs contain the restless, Romantic search for the utmost freedom of expression, but this song exists in the Classical world of joyful lightness and balance. On the basis of music alone one could easily take it for a song by Mozart.

All the same, the music is not merely square; by repeating the last words of each stanza, Schubert created a melody seven phrases long rather than six or eight. Also, the first entrance of the voice is highly unusual: a consonant appoggiatura. It is customary to sing this as a 16th note at the end of m12.

In a strophic song like this the music obviously fits the first stanza best and may or may not suit the other stanzas equally well. Imaginative changes of phrasing in later stanzas may actually improve the song and help to keep the performance interesting. For instance, in her recording of this song (Harmonia Mundi 77085–2–RG) soprano Elly Ameling combines *"Jedem lächelt traut eine Himmelsbraut"* into one legato phrase and later does the same with *". . .lächelt Laura mir einen Blick, der saget. . ."* These changes are not haphazard (Ameling does not make a habit of singing through rests), rather, they are based on an intelligent reading of the text.

Because the song remained unpublished until 1895, it was not popular until it became a favorite encore number for sopranos in the twentieth century.

Sources

Text: Hölty's version, a manuscript titled *"Minnelied"* and dated February 12, 1773, is reproduced in: *Ludwig Heinrich Christoph Hölty: Leben und Werk.* [Hannover: Schlüter, 1986.] Voss's version was published in *Gedichte*, 1783. This was the only version known to Schubert, but only lines 1 and 13 were as Hölty originally wrote them.

Music: *Franz Schubert's Werke.* Leipzig: Breitkopf und Härtel, 1895. Original key: E.

Seligkeit, D. 433

L. H. C. Hölty

Franz Schubert
(Range: E4 – G♯5)

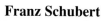

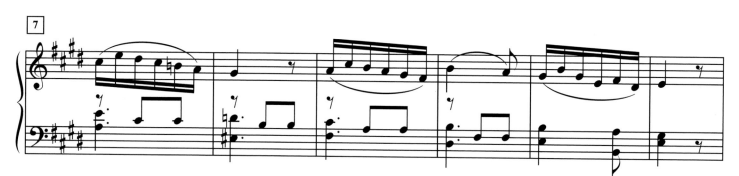

1. Freu - den son - der Zahl____ blüh'n im Him - mels -
2. Je - dem lä - chelt traut____ je - ne Him - mels -
3. Lie - ber bleib' ich hier,____ lä - chelt Lau - ra

saal!____ En - geln und__ Ver - klär - ten,
braut;____ Harf'__ und Psal - ter klin - get,
mir____ ei - nen Blick,__ der sa - get,

ⓐ "Merry." Suggestion: ♪ = ca. 190

ⓑ Sing the ornamental note as a sixteenth, ahead of the beat.

Translation: 1. Joys beyond counting bloom in the hall of Heaven! Angels and transfigured souls,
2. A heavenly bride smiles lovingly at each man; harps and psalteries are playing,
3. But I would rather stay here if only Laura would give me a glance that says

wie___ die Vä - ter lehr - ten.   O   da
und___ man tanzt___ und sin - get.   O   da
dass___ ich aus - ge - kla - get.   Se - lig

möcht' ich sein,_____ und mich e - wig
möcht' ich sein,_____ und mich e - wig
dann mit ihr,_____ bleib' ich e - wig

freun,_____ und___ mich e - wig freun!
freun,_____ und___ mich e - wig freun!
hier,_____ bleib'_ ich e - wig hier!

1. just as the Fathers taught us. O how I want to go there and be happy forever!
2. and there is dancing and singing. O how I want to go there and be happy forever!
3. my waiting is over. Then happy with her, I would stay here forever!

An die Nachtigall, D. 497

[aːn diː naxtɪɡal]

To the Nightingale

Franz Schubert (1797–1828)

eːr liːkt ʊnt ʃlɛːft aːn maenəm hɛrtsən
1. Er liegt und schläft an meinem Herzen,
He lies and sleeps by my heart

maen ɡuːtər ʃʊtsɡaest zaŋ iːn aen
2. (Mein guter Schutzgeist sang ihn ein)
my good protective-spirit sang him to-sleep

ʊnt ɪç kan frøːlɪç zaen ʊnt ʃɛrtsən
3. Und ich kann fröhlich sein und scherzen,
and I can happy be and joke,

kan jeːdər bluːm ʊnt jeːdəs blats mɪç frøøn
4. Kann jeder Blum' und jedes Blatt's mich freu'n
can every flower and every leaf myself enjoy.

naxtɪɡal naxtɪɡal ax
5. Nachtigall, Nachtigall, ach!
Nightingale, nightingale, ah!

zɪŋ miːr den aːmor nɪçt vax
6. Sing' mir den Amor nicht wach!
sing for-me (-) Love not awake!

Matthias Claudius (1740–1815)
[matiːas klaodiʊs]

Poetic Background

"Love has come to rest right on my heart, and at last I can be happy. Nightingale, do not awaken Love with your singing!" Why does the singer not want love to awaken?

The story behind the song was told by the Roman poet Apuleius. Psyche, whose name means "soul" in Greek, was so beautiful that Venus, the goddess of beauty, was jealous of her. Venus sent her son, Cupid, known as Amor in poetry, to assure that Psyche would fall in love with an ugly man. Instead, Cupid fell in love with her. In order to be with Psyche secretly, Cupid came to her only in the dark and forbade her to see him.

The poem by Claudius expresses the happiness of Psyche while Cupid (Amor) is asleep on her bosom. She knows that when he wakes up he will leave her again.

As the story continued, Psyche's curiosity drove her to light a lamp. Cupid awoke, reproached her, and fled. Psyche searched for Cupid until he took pity on her. At his request Jupiter made her immortal and allowed the two of them to marry.

Apuleius's version turned the old folk tale into an allegory of the progress of the Soul led by Love to final happiness. The story has inspired many works of art and literature.

Line 2: *Schutzgeist* did not appear in the first printed version of the poem, but rather *Engel* (angel).

Line 5: *Nachtigallen* are European songbirds, not found in America. The males sing at night during the breeding season.

Musical Background

About the time when Schubert wrote *"An die Nachtigall"* in November 1816, he moved into the home of a wealthy friend, Franz von Schober. The generosity of Schober's mother enabled Schubert to spend all his time composing. During 1816 he wrote more than 100 songs.

Schubert took the first four measures of the piano introduction from an earlier song, *"An die Geliebte"* D. 303, composed in October 1815. The text of that song begins: "O that I could kiss the tears away from your quiet eyes. . ." Perhaps the association of "quiet eyes" with the sleeping Amor led Schubert to borrow his own melody. The earlier song is musically appealing, but Claudius's far superior poem inspired Schubert to a more finely detailed song.

Compared to the Classicism of the two preceding songs in this book, the Romantic atmosphere of this song suggests much more freedom for varying the tempo. Obviously, the high note on *"Amor"* is meant to display a beautiful high, soft tone, and it may be lengthened even though there is no written rallentando in the music.

Sources

Text: *Der Wandsbecker Bothe*, May 1, 1771, p. 4. Reprinted, Hildesheim: Georg Olms, 1978. This version: *Werke*. Weimar: Utopia, 1924.

Music, autograph: Lost. First publication: [No title], Opus 98, No. 1. Vienna: Diabelli, 1829. Original key: G.

An die Nachtigall, D. 497

M. Claudius

Franz Schubert
(Range: G4 – G5)

ⓐ "Moderately." Suggestion: = ca. 86.

ⓑ Sing the appoggiatura either as an eighth note or as a quarter, replacing half or all of the note of resolution.

ⓒ Here and in measure 18 sing the appoggiatura as a 32nd note followed by a dotted 16th.

Translation: He lies asleep by my heart (my guardian angel sang him to sleep),

ⓓ No tempo change is marked, but the change to minor might suggest a slower tempo for measures 30–36.

and I can be happy and joking, I can enjoy every flower and every leaf. Nightingale, ah!, with your singing do not wake
Cupid up!

Der Tod und das Mädchen, D. 531

[der toːt ʊnt das mɛːtçən]

Death and the Maiden

Franz Schubert (1797–1828)

Das Mädchen:

forＹːbər ax   forＹːbər
1. **Vorüber! Ach, vorüber!**
Pass!   Ah,   pass!

geː   vɪldər knoxənman
2. **Geh, wilder Knochenmann!**
Go,   wild   bone-man!

ıç   bın nɔx   jʊŋ   geː liːbər
3. **Ich bin noch jung,   geh, Lieber!**
I   am still   young,   go,   dear!

ʊnt rＹːrə mıç nıçt ʔaːn
4. **Und rühre mich nicht an.**
And touch me   not   [-].

Der Tod:

giːp daene hant du: ʃøːn   ʊnt‿ tsart   gəbɪlt
5. **Gib deine Hand, du schön   und zart   Gebild!**
Give your   hand,   you beautiful and tender image!

bın frɔønd ʊnt kɔmmə nıçt‿ tsu: ʃtraːfən
6. **Bin Freund, und komme nicht, zu strafen.**
I-am friend   and   come   not   to   punish.

zae guːtəs muːts   ıç bın nıçt vılt
7. **Sei gutes Muts!   ich bin nicht wild,**
Be of-good courage! I   am not   wild;

zɔlst   zanft ın maenən armən ʃlaːfən
8. **sollst   sanft in meinen Armen schlafen!**
you-should gently in my   arms   sleep.

Matthias Claudius (1740–1815)

Poetic Background

"We fear Death, but it comes to give us pleasant rest." Two characters speak in this poem, but one singer portrays them both.

In Claudius's time Death was a more common visitor to young people than it is now. Infant mortality was many times higher because children were lost to diseases that are easily cured today. It was natural for a poet to express his grief in writing. In this poem Claudius depicts Death as a bringer of peace to someone who has been suffering and fearful. In another poem that Schubert also set to music, *"Am Grabe Anselmo's,"* (By Anselmo's Grave), D. 504, Claudius expressed his mourning for the death of a son.

Each stanza of the poem is headed with the name of the speaker. Both stanzas have the same rhyme scheme, but they contrast greatly in rhythm. The girl's stanza has short lines and a quick speaking tempo. Death's lines are longer. His speaking tempo seems to slow down from the long vowels in "*. . . schlafen. Sei gutes Muts . . .*" and even more from the uniform [ı] sound in *"ich bin nicht wild."*

Line 1: *Vorüber!* is an adverb, but it carries the meaning of a command, "Pass me by!"

Line 2: *Knochenmann*, a caricature of a skeleton, is a common image of death in religious pictures that the girl may have seen. The adjective *wilder* is in striking contrast to the peaceful voice of death that comes later.

Line 3: *Lieber* is an unexpected word, in keeping with the girl's sweetness. It says more about her than about Death.

Line 5: *schön und zart* would be *schönes und zartes* in modern German.

Line 6: *bin* lacks the subject *ich*, as if to show the egolessness of Death.

Line 7: *gutes Muts* would be *guten Muts* in modern German.

Line 8: *sollst* lacks the subject *du*, as in line 6.

Musical Background

Schubert's family also knew death well. His mother, Maria Schubert (1756–1812), bore 14 children of whom only five survived into adulthood. His father, Franz Theodor Schubert (1763–1830), married a second time and had five children of whom four survived.

The piano begins with processional music that is solemn but not extremely slow (note the *alla breve* meter signature, two beats per measure). The girl's voice enters with urgency, strongly accenting the first notes of m9 and m10. Her vocal quality must be full and emotional without heaviness. With a little slowing in mm18–22, her voice falls away. The fermata is long, and the voice of Death enters in m23 calmly, with a warm, inviting quality and perfect confidence.

It is probably not a coincidence that Schubert originally composed Death's theme in D minor. He was familiar with the climactic scene of Mozart's *Don Giovanni,* in which the statue of a murdered man, the Commendatore, comes to confront his murderer, Don Giovanni. That ghostly scene is also composed in D minor, *alla breve*, with pulsing repeated chords in the accompaniment. Despite these similarities, Mozart's and Schubert's music differs in accompaniment rhythm, in vocal range and in dynamic level. Most significantly, in this song Death's minor mode lasts only five measures; the last 17 measures are in the major mode.

Many artists have misinterpreted this song in performances and on recordings. Often both the pianist and the singer perform Death's theme at less than half of the speed that Schubert specified. Some singers have even sung Death's words with fearsome mannerisms that destroy the natural and reassuring calm that Claudius and Schubert wanted to convey.

In m37 the upper note is preferable unless one can produce a low note that is comfortable and fairly strong. If the low note sounds like a trick or an uncomfortable effort, it spoils the cumulative effect of the song.

The song was composed in February, 1817. Nearly nine years later, Schubert used Death's theme in a string quartet, D. 810, which is informally known as "Death and the Maiden." The theme appears in the second movement with the tempo marking *Andante con moto.*

Sources

Text: *Göttinger Musenalmanach 1775*, p.157. This version: Claudius. *Werke.* Weimar: Utopia, 1924, p. 131.

Music: autograph, fragments in Gesellschaft der Musikfreunde, Vienna. (Schubert's half-brother gave away pieces of the manuscript as souvenirs.) First edition: [No title], Opus 7, No. 3. Vienna: Cappi and Diabelli, 1821. Photocopy from the Hunt Library of Carnegie-Mellon University, Pittsburgh. On the last (blank) page is written in Schubert's hand, "Sch 12." Schubert initialled and numbered the copies to keep track of them because the publisher paid him a small fee for each one that was sold. Original key: D minor.

Der Tod und das Mädchen, D. 531

M. Claudius

Franz Schubert
(Range: E3 or B3 – F5)

(a) "Moderately." The metronome marking is Schubert's own. In the *String Quartet*, D. 810, known as *"Der Tod und das Mädchen,"* this theme has no metronome marking and is marked *Andante con moto* (going with motion). Both tempo markings, the metronome marking, and the *alla breve* time signature all imply warnings against too slow a tempo.

(b) "Somewhat quicker." Suggested tempo: ♩ = ca. 72.

Translation: (The Girl) Pass by, ah, pass by! Go, wild skeleton! I am still young, go away, dear one, and do not touch me.

Das erste Zeitmaß ©
Der Tod

Gib dei - ne Hand, du schön und zart Ge - bild! Bin Freund, und

kom - me nicht zu— stra - fen. Sei gu - tes Muts! ich bin nicht

wild, sollst sanft in mein - en Arm - en schla - fen!

© "The first tempo," or in Italian, *tempo primo*.

(Death) Give me your hand, you lovely and tender being! I am a friend and do not come to punish you.
Be of good cheer! I am not wild; you will gently go to sleep in my arms.

An die Musik, D. 547
[ɑːn diː muziːk]

To Music

Franz Schubert (1797–1828)

duː hɔldə kʊnst ɪn viːfiːl grɑʊən ʃtʊndən
1. **Du holde Kunst, in wieviel grauen Stunden,**
You lovely art, in how-many gray hours

voː mɪç dɛs leːbəns vɪldər kraes ʊmʃtrɪkt
2. **Wo mich des Lebens wilder Kreis umstrickt,**
in-which me (-) life's wild circle encircles

hast duː maen hɛrts tsuː varmər liːb ɛntsʊndən
3. **Hast du mein Herz zu warmer Lieb entzunden,**
have you my heart to warm love kindled,

hast mɪç ɪn aenə bɛsrə vɛlt ɛntrʏkt
4. **Hast mich in eine bess're Welt entrückt.**
have me into a better world carried-away.

ɔft hat aen zɔøftsər daenər harf ɛntflɔsən
5. **Oft hat ein Seufzer, deiner Harf' entflossen,**
Often has a sign, from-your harp escaped,

aen zyːsər haelɪgər akɔrt fɔn diːr
6. **Ein süßer, heiliger Akkord von dir,**
a sweet holy chord of yours,

den hɪmməl bɛsrər tsaetən miːr erʃlɔsən
7. **Den Himmel bess'rer Zeiten mir erschlossen,**
the heaven of-better times to-me opened-up,

duː hɔldə kʊnst ɪç daŋkə diːr dɑːfyːr
8. **Du holde Kunst, ich danke dir dafür!**
you lovely art, I thank you for-that!

Franz von Schober (1796–1882)
[frants fɔn ʃoːbər]

Poetic Background

"I am so grateful to music, the art that brings me happiness even on gray days."

We can catch the true spirit of this poem if we imagine two young men, both 20 years old, caught up in the excitement of making music. Schober could claim to be Schubert's best friend; certainly, Schubert ate many meals with the family of his high-spirited, sociable friend. Schober was certainly not a genius, but he was capable of writing appealing verses.

A further service that Schober did for Schubert was to introduce him to an important singer, Johann Michael Vogl (1768–1840). Schubert had admired Vogl's singing in the opera, where his roles included Count Almaviva in Mozart's *Le nozze di Figaro* and Pizarro in Beethoven's *Fidelio*. In February or March, 1817, Schober invited Vogl to visit him and meet Schubert. Although he did not expect to be impressed, Vogl quickly grasped the originality and craft of the 20 year old composer. Though nearing retirement from his stage career, Vogl became the most important public champion of Schubert and his songs.

Line 2: *umstrickt* lacks its auxiliary, *hat*.

Line 3: *entzunden* is archaic; modern German uses *entzündet*.

Line 5: *hat* is the auxiliary of *erschlossen* in line 7.

Musical Background

"An die Musik" was composed in March, 1817, while Schubert was still living with Schober and his mother. Slight revisions were made for the 1827 publication.

The music contains important clues to interpretation. The tempo and the meter signature are exactly the same as at the beginning of *"Der Tod und das Mädchen."* This song has no metronome marking, but it could well be the same as in the earlier song. From the beginning the bass line of the piano part has melodic interest; the left hand throughout is more important than the right hand. The frequent staccato markings in both hands require that the pedal be used lightly, not blurring the staccatos. For example, the pedal should not obliterate the staccatos in the final measures.

There is a tradition of performing this song slowly and solemnly, as if it were a farewell to music. On the contrary, it is a salute to music from two young friends who intend to go on writing songs for many years to come. The interpretive approach should be light, cheerful and full of movement.

The appoggiatura in m5 is highly unusual; it was not included in the first version of the song.

Sources

Text: autograph in Stadtbibliothek, Vienna (not included among Schober's published poems).

Music: three autographs survive of at least four that once existed. First edition: [No title], Opus 88, No. 4. Vienna: Thaddäus Weigl, 1827. Original key: D.

An die Musik, D. 547

F. von Schober

Franz Schubert

(Range: C♯4 – F♯5)

ⓐ "Moderately." Suggestion: ♩ = 54.

ⓑ Most performers sing the appoggiatura as an eighth note, but Schubert scholar Walther Dürr recommends that the appoggiatura be sung as a quarter note. (*Franz Schubert Lieder,* Heft 8. Kassel: Bärenreiter and München: G. Henle, 1982.)

Translation: 1. O lovely art, how many gray hours there have been when life's complications have encircled me, but you have kindled my heart

2. Often a sigh that flowed from your harp, one of your sweet harmonies, has opened a heaven of better

ⓒ Sing the appoggiatura as a quarter note, replacing the first printed quarter note.

ⓓ Sing the appoggiatura as a quarter note.

1. to a kindly love and lifted me up into a better world.

2. times for me. You lovely art, I thank you for that.

Lachen und Weinen, D. 777
Laughing and Weeping

Franz Schubert (1797–1828)

laxən   ʊnt vaenən tsuː jeːglıçər ʃtʊndə
1. **Lachen   und Weinen zu   jeglicher Stunde**
Laughing and weeping at   every   hour

ruːt bae der liːb ɑof zoː mançərlae grʊndə
2. **Ruht bei der Lieb' auf so   mancherlei Grunde.**
rests by (-) love on so   various   reasons.

mɔrgəns   laxt   ıç foːr lʊst
3. **Morgens   lacht' ich vor Lust;**
In-the-morning laughed I   from joy,

ʊnt varʊm ıç nuːn vaenə
4. **Und warum ich nun weine**
and why   I   now weep

bae dɛs ɑːbəndəs ʃaenə
5. **Bei des Abendes Scheine,**
at the evening's light

ıst miːr sɛlp   nıçt bəvʊst
6. **Ist mir selb' nicht bewusst.**
is to-me myself not   known.

vaenən   ʊnt laxən   tsuː jeːglıçər ʃtʊndə
7. **Weinen und Lachen zu   jeglicher Stunde**
Weeping and laughing at   every   hour

8. **Ruht bei der Lieb' auf so mancherlei Grunde.**

ɑːbənts   vaent ıç voːr ʃmɛrts
9. **Abends   weint' ich vor Schmerz;**
In-the-evening wept I   from sorrow

ʊnt varʊm duː ɛrvaxən
10. **Und warum du erwachen**
and why   you awaken

kanst am   mɔrgən mıt laxən
11. **Kannst am   Morgen mit Lachen,**
can   in-the morning with laughing,

mʊs ıç dıç frɑːgən oː hɛrts
12. **Muss ich dich fragen, o Herz.**
must I   you ask,   oh heart.

Friedrich Rückert (1788–1866)

Poetic Background

"It's puzzling. I never know when love will make me feel like laughing or crying."

In 1814 the aging poet Goethe read German translations of works by the Persian poet Hafis (1325–1389). A year later he was in love with a much younger married woman, Marianne von Willemer, and he began to write love poems to her using Persian imagery and poetic forms. These poems, including some that Marianne wrote, became *West-östlicher Diwan* (West-eastern Anthology), published in 1819.

Influenced by Goethe's poems, Rückert studied Persian and Arabic in Vienna. Rückert read Hafiz in the original Persian and began to imitate him. This poem comes from Rückert's *Östliche Rosen* (Eastern Roses), published in 1822 with a dedication to Goethe.

Title: the poem had none, so the title of the song comes from Schubert. Rückert later titled the poem *"Lachens und Weinens Grund"* (Laughing's and Crying's Reason).

Line 6: *selb'* is short for *selber*. *Bewusst* usually means "conscious," but it is used here to mean "known."

Line 10: *du* is the poet's own heart (line 12), not a second person.

Musical Background

Schubert did not date this song, which was probably written in 1822 or 1823. As in earlier periods, Schubert was again living with his friend, Schober. He had begun to publish piano music and songs, and some of his music had been performed publicly.

The form of the song is unusual: two stanzas that are parallel but varied because they dip into the minor key on the least impulse. Schubert had a phenomenal flexibility in using major and minor contrasts to respond to the nuances of poems. This aspect of his style came to full flowering in the two great song cycles *Die schöne Müllerin* (The Miller's Beautiful Daughter) and *Die Winterreise* (The Winter Journey).

The sprightly piano introduction returns between the stanzas and also afterwards, like the *ritornello* of a Baroque aria. The accidental in the piano in m11 is a subtle response to the word *weinen*. The real minor key begins in m20 while the singer is still holding the word *Lust*, as if some sorrow arises spontaneously in the heart. But the overall character of the song is optimistic and the moments of sadness are brief. The tempo remains lively throughout the song except for a slight slowing before each of the fermatas.

The pianist needs to observe the many articulation markings. As in *"An die Musik,"* over-pedalling will negate the various staccatos, portatos and accents that Schubert indicated.

Sources

Text: Rückert. *Werke,* vol. 1, page 344. Leipzig: Bibliographisches Institut, 1897.

Music: the autograph is lost. First edition: *Vier Gedichte von Rückert und Graf Platen,* Opus 59, No. 4. Vienna:

Lachen und Weinen, D. 777

F. Rückert

Franz Schubert
(Range: E♭4 – G♭5)

ⓐ "Somewhat fast." Suggestion: ♩ = ca. 108
ⓑ The irregular beaming is Schubert's.

Translation: Laughing and weeping, at whatever time of day, come from all kinds of reasons when one is in love.
This morning I was laughing for joy, and why I'm now weeping

ne   bei des A - ben-des Schei - ne,   ist mir selb' nicht be-

wusst, ist mir selb' nicht be-wusst.

Wei - nen und La - chen zu jeg - li-cher Stun - de   ruht bei der

at sunset is something I don't know myself. Weeping and laughing, at whatever time of day, come from all

ⓑ Sing the appoggiatura as either an eighth or a quarter note, replacing half or all of the first printed quarter note.

kinds of reasons when one is in love. Last evening I was weeping with pain. My heart, how can you wake up laughing?
I have to ask you, my heart!

Ständchen

[ˈʃtɛntçən]
Serenade

Franz Schubert (1797–1828)

lae̯zə fleːən maenə liːdər
1. Leise flehen meine Lieder
Softly plead my songs

dʊrç diː naxt tsuː diːr
2. Durch die Nacht zu dir;
through the night to you;

ɪn den ʃtɪllən hae̯n hɛrniːdər
3. In den stillen Hain hernieder,
into the quiet grove down-here,

liːpçən kɔm tsuː miːr
4. Liebchen, komm' zu mir!
darling, come to me!

flʏstərnt ʃlaŋkə vɪpfəl rao̯ʃən
5. Flüsternd schlanke Wipfel rauschen
Whispering slim treetops rustle

ɪn dɛs moːndəs lɪçt
6. In des Mondes Licht;
in the moon's light;

dɛs fɛrrɛːtərs fae̯ntlɪç lao̯ʃən
7. Des Verräters feindlich lauschen
the traitor's inimical listening

fʏrçtə hɔldə nɪçt
8. Fürchte, Holde, nicht!
fear, lovely-one, not!

høːrst diː naxtɪgallən ʃlaːgən
9. Hörst die Nachtigallen schlagen?
Do-you-hear the nightingales sing?

ax ziː fleːən dɪç
10. Ach! sie flehen dich,
Ah, they plead to-you,

mɪt der tøːnə zyːsən klaːgən
11. Mit der Töne süßen Klagen
with the tones' sweet complaining

fleːən ziː fyːr mɪç
12. Flehen sie für mich.
plead they for me.

ziː fɛrʃteːn dɛs buːzəns zeːnən
13. Sie verstehn des Busens Sehnen,
They understand the bosom's longing,

kɛnnən liːbəsʃmɛrts
14. Kennen Liebesschmerz,
they-know love's-pain,

ryːrən mɪt den zɪlbərtøːnən
15. Rühren mit den Silbertönen
they-move with the silver-tones

jeːdəs vae̯çə hɛrts
16. Jedes weiche Herz.
every soft heart.

las ao̯x diːr diː brust bəveːgən
17. Lass auch dir die Brust bewegen,
Let also of-you the breast be-moved,

liːpçən høːrə mɪç
18. Liebchen, höre mich!
darling, hear me;

beːbənt har ɪç diːr ɛntgeːgən
19. Bebend harr' ich dir entgegen!
trembling wait I for-you in-anticipation!

kɔm bəglʏkə mɪç
20. Komm, beglücke mich!
Come, delight me!

Ludwig Rellstab (1799–1860)
[luːtvɪç rɛlʃtaːp]

Poetic Background

"Hear my plea, beloved! Come out into the garden to me!" The image of a man singing beneath a lady's window evokes the Romantic period. Many poems, songs and instrumental works were written under the title *"Ständchen."*

In 1825 Rellstab visited Vienna and met Beethoven. He sent poems to Beethoven in the hope that they would be set to music, but they were returned to him after Beethoven died in 1827. Somehow the poems were also copied and given to Schubert. Rellstab said later that Beethoven felt too unwell to compose the poems and sent them on to Schubert as a favor, even though the two great composers had little if any contact with each other.

Line 1: *flehen* is not a verb of motion, but it takes on that role because of *durch* in line 2, giving it a close association with *fliehen* (flee) or even *fliegen* (fly).

Line 7: *Verräter* is someone who would spread scandal if he knew that the woman came out at night to meet the serenader. It is not clear why the serenader is safe from being overheard.

Line 9: *Nachtigallen* are European songbirds, not found in America. The males sing at night during the breeding season. *Schlagen* means "sing" only with reference to melodious birds, not human beings.

Line 11: *Klagen* is used because a nightingale's song is traditionally considered to be plaintive and because the pleading of an unsatisfied lover is referred to poetically as a complaint.

Line 13: *Sehnen* rhymes with *Tönen* in line 15.

Musical Background

In August, 1828, Schubert finished composing his Rellstab songs at the Schober home, where he had a music room and two other rooms for his use. His publications and many public performances of his works brought him recognition, but he was often unwell and sometimes hospitalized. In September and October Schubert lived with his brother in the suburbs, and they both went on a three-day walking trip to visit Haydn's grave at Eisenstadt. On October 31 Schubert had an attack of nausea. Thereafter he ate and drank little or nothing, but he remained somewhat active for nearly two more weeks. On about November 14 Schubert was bedridden, but friends came and played Beethoven's *String Quartet in C♯ minor*, Opus 131, at his request. On November 19 he died of typhoid fever.

In Schubert's manuscript the seven Rellstab songs are followed directly by six Heine songs. The publisher put them together with one more song and gave them the title *Schwanengesang* (Swan Song) from a legend that says a swan's ugly cry changes to a beautiful song just before death. The songs do not form a cycle but may be sung as a group, as they were first performed by Johann Michael Vogl in Vienna, January 30, 1829.

The staccatos in the introduction represent the plucking of the singer's guitar. No pedal must be used until mm 9–10, where pedal is needed to sustain the bass notes longer than they are written. Also there are parallel sixths and thirds in the treble range, as if the singer had brought along violinists to play during the interludes, add harmony (as at m21), and provide an independent obbligato on the final page.

Double grace notes occur at several points. Some authorities recommend performing them quickly and lightly on the beat, that is, simultaneously with the bass note. Others recommend performing them ahead of the beat, that is, ahead of the bass note.

Sources

Text: *Gedichte*, 1827.

Music: *Schwanengesang*, D. 957, No. 4. Autograph in the Cary Music Collection of the Pierpont Morgan Library, New York. First edition: *Schwanengesang*. Vienna: Tobias Haslinger, 1827. Original key: D minor.

Schubert's *"An die Musik"* in Schubert's handwriting, using the old German letter forms. Below the title he wrote *"Gedicht von Schober"* (poem by Schober).

With the gracious permission of the Albin Michel Publishing Company, Robert Pitrou, *Musiker der Romantik.*

Ständchen

L. Rellstab

Franz Schubert
(Range: D4 – G5)

ⓐ "Moderately." Suggestion: ♩ = ca. 70.

Translation: 1. Softly my songs plead at night to you: Darling, come down to the quiet grove.
2. Do you hear the nightingales singing? Ah, they are pleading on my behalf. With sweet complaining in their tone they plead for me.

ⓑ Sing the double grace notes quickly on the beat. Do the same in measure 21 and all subsequent cases. (Not all authorities agree.)

1. Whispering, graceful treetops are rustling in the moonlight. You need not fear that any traitor will be listening.
2. They understand the heart's longing and know love's pain; with their silver tones they move every soft heart.

nicht!

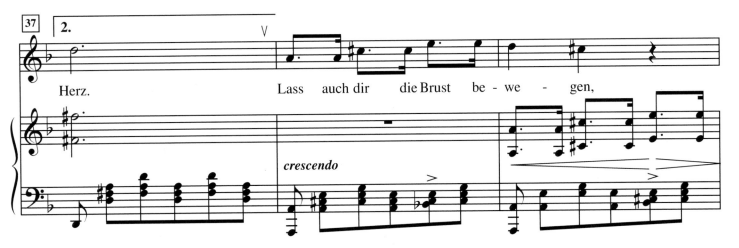

Herz.   Lass auch dir die Brust be - we - gen,

Lieb - chen, hö - re mich!   Be - bend harr'— ich

Let your heart as well be moved! Dearest, hear me! Trembling, I wait

dir ent - ge - gen!

komm, be-glü - cke

mich!

Komm, be-glü - cke mich,

be -

glü - cke mich!

decrescendo

pp

for you. Come, delight me!

Nachtwanderer

[naxtvandərər]

Night Walker

ıç vandrə dʊrç diː stɪllə naxt
1. **Ich wandre durch die stille Nacht,**
   I stroll through the quiet night,

daː ʃlaeçt der moːnt zoː haemlıç zaxt
2. **Da schleicht der Mond so heimlich sacht**
   then creeps the moon so secretly gently

ɔft aos der dʊŋklən vɔlkənhʏllə
3. **Oft aus der dunklen Wolkenhülle,**
   often from the dark cloud-cover,

ʊnt hɪn ʊnt heːr ɪm taːl
4. **Und hin und her im Tal**
   and here and there in-the valley

ɛrvaxt diː naxtɪgal
5. **Erwacht die Nachtigall,**
   awakens the nightingale,

dan viːdər alləs grao ʊnt ʃtɪllə
6. **Dann wieder alles grau und stille.**
   then again everything gray and quiet.

oː vʊndərbaːrər naxtgəzaŋ
7. **O wunderbarer Nachtgesang:**
   Oh wonderful night-song:

fɔn fɛrn ɪm lant der ʃtrøːmə gaŋ
8. **Von fern im Land der Ströme Gang,**
   from afar in-the land of rivers going,

laez ʃaoərn ɪn den dʊŋklən bɔømən
9. **Leis Schauern in den dunklen Bäumen —**
   soft shivers in the dark trees —

vɪrst diː gədaŋkən miːr
10. **Wirrst die Gedanken mir,**
    you-confuse the thoughts for-me,

maen ʔɪrrəs zɪŋən hiːr
11. **Mein irres Singen hier**
    my wandering singing here

ɪst viː aen ruːfən nuːr aos trɔømən
12. **Ist wie ein Rufen nur aus Träumen.**
    is like a calling only from dreams.

Joseph von Eichendorff (1788–1857)
[joːzɛf fɔn aeçəndɔrf]

Fanny Mendelssohn Hensel (1805–1847)
[fani mɛndəlszoːn hɛnzəl]

Poetic Background

"As I walked alone at night, the sights and sounds left me with confused thoughts and a feeling that my own songs are unreal."

Eichendorff's poem tests the line between rational and irrational uses of language and, therefore, between aspects of his own mind. In Romantic imagery night is a time of either wakefulness or dreams. Here the poet is wakeful, wandering outdoors at night with no other stated purpose but to observe the sights and sounds of nature.

The first stanza is primarily factual, descriptive; the second reaches into the poet's emotional depths. The poet addresses not the nightingale, but its plaintive song, combined with other sounds of the night. They confuse his thoughts and make him feel that his own poetry (*Singen*) is rambling (*irr*); it is only a calling out (*Rufen*) based on unreality (*Träumen*). Faced with the profundity of night's song, the poet passes a harsh judgment on his own talent.

The content of the poem is strikingly reflected in the form. Imagery of quietness and a stately tempo predominate in each of the two six-line stanzas, except that the fourth and fifth lines of each stanza are shorter and introduce elements of restlessness.

Title: Hensel used the 1837 edition of Eichendorff's poems, in which two poems are together under the title *"Nachtwanderer."* In later editions this poem has its own title, *"Nachts."*

Lines 3 and 9: *dunklen*; Hensel used *dunkeln*, whether by choice or accident.

Line 5: *Nachtigallen* are European songbirds, not found in America. The males sing at night during the breeding season.

Line 10 and 11: *wirrst. . . irres*, Hensel used *irrst. . . wirres*, obviously in error.

Musical Background

This marvelous song, completed on June 15, 1843, displays Hensel at the peak of her powers as a lied composer. Beginning with a melody in the piano accompanied by warm, dark chords, the voice and piano have interwoven melodies throughout. (Hensel may have learned this technique from Schumann, who used it often.) Dovetailed with the last note of the first stanza, the piano begins the melody of the second stanza in m17. Tremolos build tension; at m23 the measures become shorter and the melody breaks into excited fragments. At m34 both voice and piano resume their former calm, but the poet's sadness pours out in the diminished seventh slur of the next to last syllable. Finally, the song ends as calmly as it began; the night is undisturbed.

Hensel found a noteworthy harmonic inspiration to express the emotionally intense word *"Träumen."* At the end of m36 there is a fully diminished seventh chord; in m37 the third of the chord is lowered, resulting in a chord of the diminished third. When the chord changes on beat 4 of m37, the lowered tone is sustained in the voice. The dissonant tone is a minor ninth above the bass but the voice leaps away from the dissonance without resolving it. (Hensel's brother never wrote anything as harmonically daring as this measure.)

Hensel was a brilliant pianist who mastered every technique of her time. In mm27–29 especially, she wrote notes that most hands cannot reach, but she either played them or created the illusion. Tremolos of two or more notes were much in favor in her generation, but the effect may not be convincing on modern pianos that have a heavier action and deeper resonance. Depending on the available instrument and on the pianist's technique, it may be advisable in the three-note chords to sustain the upper note and alternate only the two lower ones.

Hensel's rhythmic notation in mm 26–31 was ambiguous, showing a signature of 6/8 with note values and use of beams appropriate for 3/4 time. *L'istesso tempo* means that the eighth-note remains steady through the changes.

Sources

Text: *Aus dem Leben eines Taugenichts und das Marmorbild. Zwei Novellen nebst einem Anhange von Liedern und Romanzen.* Berlin: Vereinsbuchhandlung, 1826. (The lengthy title of the book indicates that it contains two long stories, "From the Life of a Good-for-Nothing" and "The Marble Image," and a supplement of 48 poems described as "songs and romances.") This version: *Werke.* München: Winkler-Verlag, 1970, p. 49.

Music: *Sechs Lieder*, Opus 7, No. 1. Berlin: Bote & Bock, 1847. Reprinted, 1985. Original key: F.

Nachtwanderer

J. von Eichendorff

Fanny Mendelssohn Hensel
(Range: C4 - F5)

ⓐ Suggestion: ♩. = ca. 48.

Translation: I walk outdoors in the quiet night; the moon slips out so quietly

from behind its cover of dark clouds. And here and there in the valley a nightingale wakes up, then everything returns again to grayness and silence. O

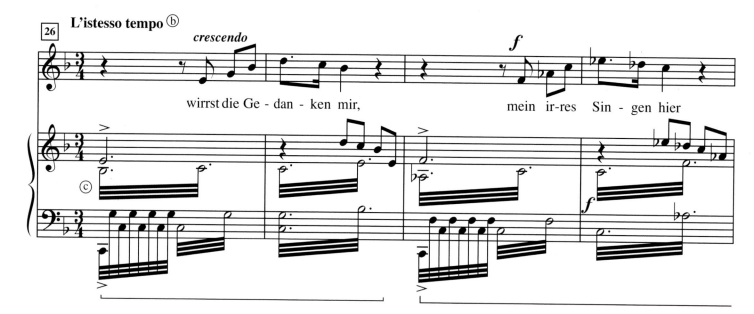

ⓑ "The same tempo." The eighth note remains constant, resulting in a new tempo of ♩=ca. 72. Hensel used a meter signature of 6/8 here, but the note values and beams require a signature of 3/4.

ⓒ The first edition erroneously showed only four 32nd notes on beat one; the fifth through eighth notes have been added here to regularize the rhythm. The same correction has been made to m28 and m30.

marvelous night song from far away in the land where streams flow, quiet shiver in the dark trees, you confuse my thoughts; my aimless singing here

ⓓ In the first edition the voice part has the dynamics shown here, but the piano part has: (m34) no crescendo, but *p* on beat 7; (m35) a crescendo on beat 4; and (m36) no dynamic marking. It seems advisable for the piano to follow the dynamics of the voice.

is merely a crying out in the midst of dreams.

Kommen und Scheiden

[ˈkɔmmən ʊnt ˈʃaedən]
Coming and Parting

Fanny Mendelssohn Hensel (1805–1847)

zoː ɔft ziː kɑːm ɛrˈʃiːn miːr diː ɡəˈʃtalt
1. **So   oft   sie kam, erschien mir   die Gestalt**
However often she came, seemed   to-me the appearance

zoː ˈliːplɪç viː das ˈeːrstə ɡryːn ɪm valt
2. **So lieblich, wie das erste grün im   Wald.**
as   lovely   as   the first   green in-the forest.

ʊnt was ziː ʃprɑːx draŋ   miːr tsʊm ˈhɛrtsən ʔaen
3. **Und was sie sprach, drang   mir zum Herzen ein**
And what she spoke   penetrated me   to-the heart   in

zyːs   viː dɛs ˈfryːlɪŋs ˈeːrstəs liːt ɪm haen
4. **Süß,   wie des Frühlings erstes Lied im   Hain.**
sweetly as   the spring's   first   song in-the grove.

ʊnt als ˈleːpvoːl ziː ˈvɪŋktə mɪt der hant
5. **Und als Lebwohl sie winkte mit der Hand,**
And as   farewell   she waved with the hand,

vaːrs ɔp   der ˈlɛtstə ˈjuːɡəntˌtraom miːr   ʃvant
6. **War's, ob   der letzte Jugendtraum mir   schwand.**
was-it as-if the last   youth-dream   from-me disappeared.

Nikolaus Lenau (1802–1850)
[ˈnɪkolaos ˈleːnao]

Poetic Background

"I was fascinated by her, and when she waved goodbye, my dream of happiness ended."

Lenau tended to a melancholy outlook all his life. Formative elements in his life were: a deep attachment to his widowed mother; playing the violin; an unhappy love affair; and awareness that others in his family had suffered from depression. Lenau was a friend of Wilhelm Hensel before the latter's marriage to Fanny Mendelssohn.

This brief but heartfelt poem, written in 1840, is found in Lenau's second volume of poetry in the section entitled *Liebesklänge* (Love's Sounds). Lenau wrote it in three stanzas, each of which is a rhymed couplet of iambic pentameter.

Line 1: *Gestalt* has many connotations, including character, form and appearance.

Line 5: *Lebwohl* is understood to mean goodbye forever. That she "waved" goodbye hints that the parting did not seem tragic to her, only to the poet.

Line 6: *ob* stands for *als ob* (as if). *Schwand* is past tense of *schwinden*.

Musical Background

Hensel completed this song on December 27, 1846, less than five months before she died.

Although the song makes an initial impression of simplicity, its poignancy is produced by Hensel's subtle, masterly modulations. The first couplet carries the song from tonic key to the dominant, and Hensel repeats the couplet to extend the dominant. The second couplet begins in the supertonic key and modulates back to the tonic. The third couplet is in the tonic minor and uses the poignant Neapolitan harmony in m43. The major mode returns in a short coda, a mere reminiscence of the happiness the poet once felt.

Hensel's manuscript shows that she first wrote measures 20 and 21 as they appear here but then crossed them out. Perhaps they should not be performed, but it is interesting to see what her original idea was. I therefore include the two measures with the syllables *"vi-"* and *"-de,"* a traditional way of marking a cut.

Robert Schumann also set this poem to music in 1850 (Opus 90, No. 3). Hensel's song was unpublished, hence Schumann was probably unaware of it.

Sources

Text: *Sämtliche Werke*. Leipzig: Hesse & Becker, no date (early 1900s).

Music: Mendelssohn Archive Manuscript (MA Ms) 49, pages 136–137, in the Deutsche Staatsbibliothek, Berlin. First publication in *16 Songs* by Fanny Mendelssohn Hensel, edited by John Glenn Paton. Van Nuys: Alfred, 1995. Original key: A.

Kommen und Scheiden

N. Lenau

Fanny Hensel
(Range: E4 – F♯5)

ⓐ Suggestion: ♩· = ca. 63

Translation: Whenever she came, her being seemed to me as lovely as the first green leaves in the woods.

kam,_____ er - schien mir die Ge - stalt_____ so lieb - lich, so

lieb - lich, wie___ das er - ste Grün im Wald.

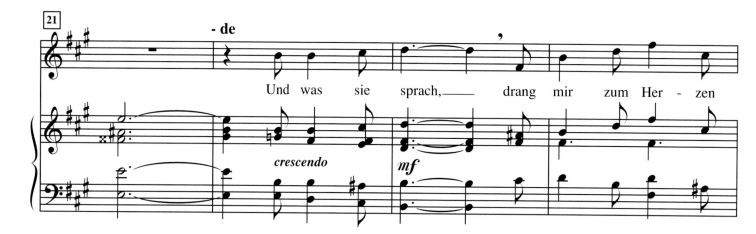

- de

Und was sie sprach,_____ drang mir zum Her - zen

crescendo mf

ein_____ süß, wie des Früh - lings

And all that she said penetrated into my heart as sweetly as spring's

er - stes Lied___ im Hain,___ süß, wie des

Früh - lings er - stes Lied___ im Hain.

Und als Leb - wohl___ sie wink - te mit der

Hand,___ war's, ob der letz - te Ju - gend-traum mir

ⓑ Sing the ornamental note quickly, before the beat.

first song in the grove. And when she waved farewell with her hand, it was as if my last youthful dream

schwand,— und als Leb - wohl_____ sie wink - te mit der

Hand,_____ war's,— ob der letz - te Ju - gend - traum_____ mir

schwand, als ob der letz - te

Ju - gend - traum mir schwand._____

disappeared.

Jagdlied
[ˈjɑːktliːt]
Hunting Song

Felix Mendelssohn (1809–1847)
[ˈfeːlɪks ˈmɛndəlszoːn]

mɪt lʊst tɛːt ɪç ˈɑosraetən
1. Mit Lust tät ich ausreiten
With joy did I ride-out

dʊrç ˈaenən ˈgryːnən valt
2. Durch einen grünen Wald,
through a green forest.

daˈrɪn dɑː høːrt ɪç ˈzɪŋən
3. Darin da hört' ich singen
Therein then heard I singing

drae ˈføːglaen ˈvoːləʃtalt
4. Drei Vöglein wohlgestalt.
three little-birds of-good-appearance.

ʊnt zɪnt ɛs nɪçt drae ˈføːgəlaen
5. Und sind es nicht drei Vögelein,
And are they not three little-birds,

zoː zɪnts drae ˈfrɔølaen faen
6. So sind's drei Fräulein fein,
so are-they three young-women fine.

zɔl miːr das aen nɪçt ˈveːrdən
7. Soll mir das Ein' nicht werden,
Should mine the one not become,

zoː gɪlts das ˈleːbən maen
8. So gilt's das Leben mein.
so it's-worth the life mine.

di ˈɑːbəntʃtrɑːlən ˈbraetən
9. Die Abendstrahlen breiten
The evening-rays spread

das ˈgɔltnɛts ˈyːbərn valt
10. Das Goldnetz übern Wald,
the gold-net over-the forest,

ʊnt iːm ɛntˈgeːgən ˈʃtraetən
11. Und ihm entgegen streiten
and it toward compete

di ˈføːglaen das ɛs ʃalt
12. Die Vöglein, dass es schallt.
the little-birds, so-that it rings.

ɪç ˈʃteːə ɑof der ˈlɑoər
13. Ich stehe auf der Lauer,
I stand on the lookout,

ɪç hɑr ɑof ˈdʊŋklə naxt
14. Ich harr' auf dunkle Nacht,
I listen to dark night.

ɛs hat der ˈɑːbənt.ʃɑoər
15. Es hat der Abendschauer
There has the evening-shower

iːr hɛrts voːl vaeç gəˈmaxt
16. Ihr Herz wohl weich gemacht.
her heart indeed soft made.

ɪns ˈjuːbəlhɔrn ɪç ˈstoːsə
17. In's Jubelhorn ich stoße,
Into-the rejoicing-horn I blow:

das ˈfɪrmamɛnt vɪrt klɑːr
18. Das Firmament wird klar,
the firmament becomes bright.

ɪç ˈʃtaegə fɔn dem ˈrɔsə
19. Ich steige von dem Rosse,
I climb-down from the horse

ʊnt tseːl diː ˈføːgəlʃɑːr
20. Und zähl die Vögelschaar.
and count the birds-crowd.

di ʔaen ɪst ˈʃvartsbrɑon ˈʔannə
21. Die Ein' ist schwarzbraun' Anne,
The one is brunette Anne,

di ˈʔandrə ˈbɛrbəlaen
22. Die Andre Bärbelein,
the second little-Barbara,

di drɪt hat ˈkaenən ˈnɑːmən
23. Die Dritt' hat keinen Namen,
the third has no name,

di zɔl maen ˈʔaegən zaen
24. Die soll mein eigen sein.
that-one shall my own be.

Achim von Arnim (1781–1831)
[ˈaxɪm fɔn ˈarnɪm]

Poetic Background

"Out for a day of hunting, I was soon on the trail of three young women who were heard singing. I spent the night in the woods, and in the morning I found them. The nameless one is the one that I'm determined to marry."

Arnim and his friend Clemens Brentano assembled a collection of German folk poetry that had enormous influence other poets, composers and painters. They diligently researched books, periodicals and song sheets to find texts from the previous 300 years. They aimed to renew German poetry by reconnecting it with long forgotten roots in the texts of popular songs. Their imaginative title, *Des Knaben Wunderhorn* (The Boy's Magic Horn), combines the image of youth with outdoor music making, although they were not musicians and dealt only with poetic texts.

Enthusiasts but not scholars, Arnim and Brentano had no inhibitions about re-writing the old poems. Arnim called this one *"Nächtliche Jagd"* (Nocturnal Hunt). He described its source only as *"mündlich"* (oral), but he took it from various early books and added lines 9–20, which are purely his own. His version has four eight-line stanzas; Mendelssohn used only the first three.

Line 1: *tät* is an archaic form of *tat*, the past tense of *tun*. The combination of *tun* (to do) with an infinitive can still be heard in conversation.

Line 8: *gilt's*, or *gilts* in the poem, is a contraction of *es gilt*, from the verb *gelten* (to be worth). The idiom means, "I would bet my life on her becoming mine."

Line 21: *schwarzbraun* is a common expression for a dark complexion with brown eyes.

Line 24: *des Jägers* is the old form; Mendelssohn changed it to *mein eigen* (my own).

Musical Background

"Jagdlied" was composed in 1834 while Mendelssohn was employed as a conductor by the city of Düsseldorf. He conducted major oratorios and operas during his two year contract.

The German forest with all of its Romantic aura is summoned up by the sound of hunting horns, circular, valveless instruments that are played by groups of outdoor sportsmen. The open fifths heard in mm30–33 are a harmonic cliché known as "horn fifths," used in imitation of the musical style of a group of hunting horns. The vocal line is also influenced by horn style, staying mostly on pitches that would be available on a natural horn.

Notice that Mendelssohn asked for a moderate tempo and for gentle dynamics, even at the end. The singer's last phrase is a wish, not a triumph. After two stanzas of steady tempo, the fermatas in the third stanza put a frame of thoughtfulness around the words "the third has no name." Approach both fermatas in strict tempo, with no slowing beforehand. Be sure that the pedal is lifted after each fermata to avoid an unwanted connection with the next phrase.

"Jagdlied" was completed on May 25, 1834, but published posthumously.

Mendelssohn probably did not know the Renaissance melody to which these words were sung in polyphonic settings by Ludwig Senfl (1534), Caspar Othmayr (1549), and Orlando di Lasso (1583). (Details and the tune can be found in *Deutscher Liederhort* by Erk und Böhme, 1893). Brahms altered the tune slightly in his version for four part chorus in *Deutsche Volkslieder* (1864).

Sources

Text: *Des Knaben Wunderhorn: alte deutsche Lieder*, vol. 1. Heidelberg: Mohr und Zimmer, 1806 (actually 1805). Reprinted, Leipzig: Insel, 1910. (Details about sources are given by Ferdinand Rieser in *"Des Knaben Wunderhorn" und seine Quellen*. Dortmund: Ruhfus, 1908.)

Music, first edition: *Drei Lieder*, Opus 84, no. 3. 1850. Original key: E.

Jagdlied

16th century, altered by A. von Arnim

Felix Mendelssohn
(Range: D4 – G5)

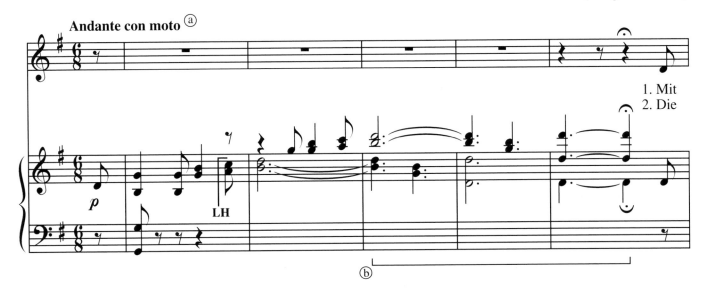

ⓐ Suggestion: ♩. = ca. 96

ⓑ The pedal marking is Mendelssohn's. Be sure to clear the pedal before playing the upbeat to m6.

Translation: 1. I rode out happily through a green wood, where I heard three
2. The late sun spreads golden rays over the wood; the

1. beautiful birds singing. And if it wasn't three birds, it was three fine young women. I must have one of them; I'd bet my life on it.

2. little birds are trying to outdo one another. I'm watchful, listening into the deep night. An evening shower has surely made their hearts soft.

I blow joyfully into my hunting horn as the sky grows brighter. I climb down from my horse and take a count of the group of birds.

Ein' ist schwarz - braun' An - ne, die And - re Bär - be - lein, die

Dritt' hat kei - nen Na - men, die soll mein ei - gen

crescendo

sein, _____ mein ei - gen sein, _____ die

crescendo

diminuendo

soll mein ei - gen sein.

p

pp

One is dark-haired Anna, another is Barbara. The third has no name; she is just right for me.

Auf Flügeln des Gesanges
On Wings of Song

Felix Mendelssohn (1809–1847)

ɑof flyːgəln dɛs gəzɑŋəs
1. **Auf Flügeln des Gesanges,**
   On   wings   of   song,

hɛrtsliːpçən   trɑːg ɪç   dɪç   fɔrt
2. **Herzliebchen, trag' ich dich fort,**
   heart-darling,   carry I   you   away,

fɔrt   nax   den fluːrən   dɛs   gɑŋəs
3. **Fort nach den Fluren   des   Ganges,**
   away to   the   fertile-plains of-the Ganges;

dɔrt   vaes   ɪç   den ʃøːnstən   ɔrt
4. **Dort weiß ich den schönsten   Ort.**
   there know I   the   most-beautiful place.

dɔrt   liːkt aen roːtblyːəndərgartən
5. **Dort liegt ein rotblühender Garten**
   There lies   a   red-blooming garden

ɪm   ʃtɪllən moːndənʃaen
6. **Im   stillen Mondenschein;**
   in-the quiet   moonlight;

diː   loːtɔsbluːmən   ɛrvɑrtən
7. **Die Lotosblumen   erwarten**
   the lotus-flowers   await

iːr   trɑotəs ʃvɛstərlaen
8. **Ihr trautes Schwesterlein.**
   their intimate little-sister.

diː   faelçən   kɪçərn   ʊnt   koːzən
9. **Die Veilchen kichern und kosen,**
   The violets   giggle   and   caress,

ʊnt   ʃɑon   nax   den ʃtɛrnən ɛmpoːr
10. **Und schau'n nach den Sternen empor;**
    and   gaze   to   the   stars   upward;

haemlɪç   ɛrtsɛːlən diː roːzən
11. **Heimlich erzählen die Rosen**
    secretly   tell   the   roses

zɪç   dʊftəndə mɛːrçən ɪns   oːr
12. **Sich   duftende Märchen in's   Ohr.**
    each-other fragrant   fairy-tales in-the ear.

ɛs   hʏpfən hɛrbae ʊnt   lɑoʃən
13. **Es   hüpfen herbei und lauschen**
    There hop   near   and   listen

diː   frɔmmən kluːgən gatsɛln
14. **Die frommen, klugen Gazell'n;**
    the   docile,   cunning gazelles,

ʊnt   ɪn der fɛrnə   rɑoʃən
15. **Und in der Ferne   rauschen**
    and   in the distance roar

dɛs haelgən ʃtroːməs vɛln
16. **Des heil'gen Stromes Well'n.**
    the   holy   river's   currents.

dɔrt   vɔllən viːr niːdərzɪŋkən
17. **Dort wollen wir niedersinken**
    There want   we   to-sink-down

ʊntər dem palmənbɑom
18. **Unter dem Palmenbaum,**
    under the   palm-tree

ʊnt li:b   ʊnt ruːə trɪŋkən
19. **Und Lieb' und Ruhe trinken**
    and love   and quiet   drink

ʊnt trɔømən seːlɪgən trɑom
20. **Und träumen seligen   Traum.**
    and dream   blessed   dream.

Heinrich Heine (1797–1856)
[haenrɪç haenə]

Poetic Background

"My songs will carry you away to an exotic dreamland."

After Goethe revealed his interest in Persian poetry, other poets also looked eastward. Heine became sensitive to ideas and topics from India through his studies with August von Schlegel in Bonn in 1821. He used Indian motives in this poem, *"Die Lotosblume"* and several others. In a collection of stories entitled *Die Serapionsbrüder* E. T. A. Hoffmann used the phrase "wings of song." Heine mentioned in a letter that he had read the book, but he did not say whether he intentionally had borrowed the phrase for his own poem.

Heine wrote this poem around December 1822. In the following year he included it in a book with the ungainly title, *Tragedies, with a Lyrical Intermezzo.* The tragedies were two plays in verse. Heine borrowed the theatrical idea of a lighter intermezzo between two heavier pieces (intermezzo is also used for an instrumental piece between acts of an opera). Later, when the tragedies had been forgotten, Heine still kept the name *Lyrical Intermezzo* for the group of poems, even though there were no heavier works surrounding it. This poem is the ninth in the group of 65 short lyrics, which includes his most famous poems.

Line 5: *rotblühender Garten,* as Heine acknowledged, came from a Sanskrit play by Kalidasa (5th century), translated into German by Forster, 1791.

Line 9: *Die Veilchen . . .* In December 1821 Heine wrote a letter to a friend who had studied with him in Bonn and playfully compared himself and others to plants: "I believe I was then a waterlily and fell in love with a violet. You were then a broad-leafed palm and often rustled over our heads when I and my violet played together. . ."

Line 14: *fromm*, applied to persons means "pious," applied to animals means "docile."

Line 16: *heil'gen* is shortened from Heine's word *heiligen*. *Stromes* refers to the Ganges, which is considered a holy river. *Wellen*, usually translated "waves," often describes the rippling waters of a river in German poetry.

Line 19: *Lieb'* in earlier editions of the poem, *Liebe* in later versions.

Musical Background

Violinists have performed this famous melody at least as often as singers. While many songs demand to be brought to life dramatically, the singer's challenge here is to perform the melody as perfectly and expressively as we would expect of a fine instrumentalist.

Sources

Text: *Tragödien, nebst einem lyrischen Intermezzo.* Berlin, 1823. *Lyrisches Intermezzo* was also a section of *Buch der Lieder*, 1827. This version: *Heine Säkularausgabe, Gedichte, 1812–1827*, vol. 1. Ed., Hans Böhm. Berlin: Akademie-Verlag, 1979.

Music, first edition: *Sechs Lieder*, Opus 34, No. 2. 1836. Original key: A♭.

Auf Flügeln des Gesanges

H. Heine

Felix Mendelssohn
(Range: E♭4 – F5)

ⓐ Suggestion: ♩. = ca. 50

Translation: 1. On wings of song, heart's darling, I will carry you away to the plains
2. The violets giggle and caress and look up at the stars; secretly the roses tell

(b) Grace notes, here and elsewhere, are sung quickly and before the beat.

(c) Double grace notes, here and elsewhere, are sung as sixteenths on the third beat.

1. of the Ganges, where I know the loveliest place. There is a garden of red flowers under quiet moonlight; the lotuses are waiting for their

2. fragrant stories to each other. The docile, cunning gazelles hop near to listen, and in the distance one hears the sound of the

16 / **41**

diminuendo *p*

trau - tes Schwes - ter - lein, ____ die Lo - tos - blu - men er -

diminuendo *p*

heil' - gen Stro - mes Well'n, ____ und in der Fer - ne

diminuendo *pp*

19 / **44**

crescendo , *p*

war ____ ten ihr trau - tes Schwes - ter - lein.

crescendo , *p*

rau ____ schen des heil' - gen Stro - mes Well'n.

p *crescendo*

23 **1.**

f *diminuendo*

1. dear sister.
2. holy river.

2. Die

3. Dort wol - len wir nie - der -

sin - ken   un - ter dem Pal - men - baum,   und

Lieb' und Ru - he trin - ken und träu - men se - li - gen

Traum,_____ und träu - men

3. There we will sink down under a palm tree and drink in love and quiet and dream a blessed dream.

se - li - gen Traum,

diminuendo

sel' - gen Traum.

"Auf Flügeln des Gesanges" in Mendelssohn's handwriting, using the old German letter forms. The song is titled *"Abendlied"* (Evening Song), but that title was not used when the song was published.

With the gracious permission of the Albin Michel Publishing Company, Robert Pitrou, *Musiker der Romantik.*

Nachtlied

[naxtliːt]

Night Song

Felix Mendelssohn (1809–1847)

fɛrgaŋən ɪst der lɪçtə taːk
1. **Vergangen ist der lichte Tag,**
   Past   is   the bright day;

fɔn fɛrnə kɔmt der glɔkən ʃlaːk
2. **Von ferne kommt der Glocken Schlag;**
   from afar comes the bells'   stroke.

zoː raest diː tsaet diː gantsə naxt
3. **So reist die Zeit die ganze Nacht,**
   So travels the time the whole night—

nɪmt mançən mɪt ders nɪçt gədaxt
4. **Nimmt manchen mit, der's nicht gedacht.**
   takes some   along, who-it not thought.

voː ɪst nuːn hɪn diː bʊntə lʊst
5. **Wo ist nun hin die bunte Lust,**
   Where is now gone the colorful joy,

dɛs frɔøndəs troːst ʊnt trɔøə brʊst
6. **Des Freundes Trost und treue Brust,**
   the friend's comfort and faithful breast,

der liːpstən zyːsər ʔaogənʃaen
7. **Der Liebsten süßer Augenschein?**
   the beloved's sweet eye-light?

vɪl kaenər mɪt miːr mʊntər zaen
8. **Will keiner mit mir munter sein?**
   Will no-one with me cheerful be?

frɪʃ ʔaof dɛn liːbə naxtɪgal
9. **Frisch auf denn, liebe Nachtigall,**
   Fresh up then, dear nightingale,

duː vasərfall mɪt hɛlləm ʃal
10. **Du Wasserfall mit hellem Schall!**
    you waterfall with bright sound,

gɔt loːbən vɔllən viːr fɛrʔaent
11. **Gott loben wollen wir vereint,**
    God to-praise want we unified

bɪs das der lɪçtə mɔrgən ʃaent
12. **Bis dass der lichte Morgen scheint!**
    until that the bright morning shines.

Joseph von Eichendorff (1788–1857)

Poetic Background

"Alone at night, away from all human friends, I devote these hours to praising God."

In his twenties Eichendorff wrote a semi-autobiographical novel, *Ahnung und Gegenwart* (Premonition and Presence). It contains more than 50 lyric poems, usually introduced as occasions when characters sing, alone or in groups.

In one scene of the novel the central character Friedrich is passing the night in the castle of a mysterious, seductive woman. Awakening during the night, he hears his friend Leontin singing this poem outdoors in solitude. Friedrich arises and finds his friend, and they go away together.

The poem has five stanzas, of which Mendelssohn used the first, second and fifth.

Line 2: *Glockenschlag* may be the hourly ringing of the clock in a church tower or it may be a small tolling bell that is rung in churches when a parishioner is dying. The latter is suggested by the persistence of the repeated dominant tone through much of the song.

Line 6: *Der Liebsten* is either feminine or plural possessive, that is, either "the beloved woman's" or "the dearest ones'." The poem has instead *"Des Weibes . . ."* (womankind's). The word *Augenschein* is Eichendorff's invention, meaning "light of the eye."

Line 9: *Frisch auf* is an idiom, now somewhat old fashioned, that means "Let's be off" or "Let's go." *Nachtigall* is a European songbird, not found in America. The males sing at night during the breeding season.

Line 10: *Wasserfall*, a bold poetic image, calling the bird a "cascade of bright sound."

Musical Background

Mendelssohn wrote this song, one of his most deeply felt works, on October 1, 1847. He was still grieving for his sister Fanny, who on May 14 had suddenly died of a stroke. Mendelssohn also had a stroke at the end of October; he died at home in Leipzig on November 4 at the age of 38. Schumann and other famous musicians were his pallbearers, and he was widely mourned, especially in Germany and England.

Despite its serious and sacred nature, *"Nachtlied"* is deeply affirmative in its message. That the composer chose this particular text in a time of personal grief is a testimony to his positive personal faith. The song constitutes a statement of faith that rises above both loneliness and fear of death.

Sources

Text, first edition: *Ahnung und Gegenwart*, written 1811, published 1815. This version: *Werke*. München: Winkler-Verlag, 1970, p.286.

Music, first edition: *Sechs Lieder*, Opus 71, No. 6. Original key: E♭.

Nachtlied

J. von Eichendorff

Felix Mendelssohn
(Range D4 – A♭5)

Ver - gan - gen ist der lich - te Tag, von

fer - ne kommt der Glo - cken Schlag; so reist die Zeit die gan - ze Nacht,

nimmt man - chen mit, der's nicht ge - dacht. Wo

ⓐ Suggestion: ♪ = ca. 76

Translation: The light of day is gone; in the distance a bell rings. So time passes all night, taking some away who never expected it.

What became of bright joy, the comfort of faithful friends, the light of loved ones' eyes? Is there no cheerful person to keep me company? Then let us join together, dear nightingale, you cascade of beautiful song— let us praise God

eint,   bis   dass   der   lich - te   Mor - gen   scheint,

diminuendo

Gott   lo - ben   wol - len   wir   ver - eint,

p   *crescendo*

bis   dass   der   lich - te   Mor - gen

p   *pp*

scheint.

pp

together until the light of morning appears.

Widmung

['vɪtmʊŋ]

Dedication

Robert Schumann (1810–1856)

[ˈroːbɛrt ˈʃuːman]

du: ˈmaenə ˈzeːlə du: maen hɛrts
1. Du meine Seele, du mein Herz,
You my soul, you my heart,

du: ˈmaenə vɔn oː du: maen ʃmɛrts
2. Du meine Wonn', o du mein Schmerz,
you my joy, oh you my pain,

du: ˈmaenə vɛlt ɪn deːr ɪç ˈleːbə
3. Du meine Welt, in der ich lebe,
you my world, in which I live,

maen ˈhɪmməl du: ˈdaraen ɪç ˈʃveːbə
4. Mein Himmel du, darein ich schwebe,
my heaven you, in which I soar

oː du: maen graːp ɪn das ˈhɪnap
5. O du mein Grab, in das hinab
oh you, my grave, into which downward

ɪç ˈeːvɪç ˈmaenən ˈkʊmmər gaːp
6. Ich ewig meinen Kummer gab!
I for-eternity my grief gave!

du: bɪst di: ruː du: bɪst der ˈfriːdən
7. Du bist die Ruh', du bist der Frieden,
You are (-) rest, you are (-) peace,

du: bɪst der ˈhɪmməl miːr bəˈʃiːdən
8. Du bist der Himmel mir beschieden.
you are the heaven to-me granted.

das du: mɪç liːpst maxt mɪç miːr weːrt
9. Dass du mich liebst, macht mich mir wert,
That you me love makes me to-myself worthy;

daen blɪk hat mɪç foːr miːr verˈklɛːrt
10. Dein Blick hat mich vor mir verklärt,
your gaze has me before myself transfigured.

du: heːpst mɪç ˈliːbənt ˈyːbər mɪç
11. Du hebst mich liebend über mich,
You raise me lovingly above myself,

maen ˈguːtər gaest maen ˈbɛsrəs ɪç
12. Mein guter Geist, mein bess'res Ich!
my good spirit, my better I!

Friedrich Rückert (1788–1866)

Poetic Background

"You are everything to me. Your love gives my life meaning and lifts me above my normal self."

Inspired by his new bride, Luise Wiethaus, Rückert poured out his feelings in poems that are enriched by his profound study of Middle Eastern languages. (For more information, read about *"Lachen und Weinen"* on page 49.) The resulting book, *Liebesfrühling* (Springtime of Love), has been called "a catechism for lovers" because it explores so many facets of romantic love. Its five sections, each called a *Strauß* (bouquet), have titles that tell a story: *Erwacht, Geschieden, Gemieden, Wiedergewonnen, Verbunden* (Awakened, Parted, Avoided, Won Again, United). The individual poems have no titles; this poem is the third one in *Erwacht.*

Line 1: *Du meine Seele* and the following phrases are all terms of address; the first main verb, *bist*, is found in line 7.

Line 2: *Du meine Wonn', o du. . .* is Schumann's word change for the sake of the enthusiastic *"o."* Rückert wrote, *"Du meine Wonne, du. . . ,"* which is consistent with line 1.

Line 5: *Grab* is an unusual image in a love song; perhaps Rückert is thinking that his ego dies in his love.

Line 8: *der Himmel* is Rückert's phrase, meaning "You are the Heaven granted to me." Schumann accidentally changed it to *"vom Himmel. . ."* (from Heaven), meaning "You are granted to me from Heaven." Clara Schumann regarded *"der"* as correct and *"vom"* as a mistake. (See C. V. Bos, *The Well Tempered Accompanist.* Bryn Mawr: Theodore Presser, 1949.)

Musical Background

Schumann called this song "Dedication" because it opens the book of songs that he created as a wedding gift for his bride, Clara Wieck. The songs were composed in the spring of 1840 but were kept secret until September 11, the evening before the wedding. At Schumann's request the publisher had prepared a special leatherbound copy for Clara.

Schumann named the book *Myrthen* [ˈmyrtən] (myrtles) after an evergreen shrub, one of many in the myrtle family. Many myrtles contain fragrant oils and also bear flowers; perhaps that was sufficient reason for Schumann to call his songs "myrtles." Both he and Clara must also have remembered that the final song of his *Liederkreis,* Opus 24, is a poem by Heine that speaks of decorating a book of poems *mit Myrthen und Rosen* (with myrtles and roses).

Because no single voice would suit all of the songs — songs 5 and 6 were originally notated in bass clef — *Myrthen* is not suited to be sung as a song cycle. Schumann gave the book some unity by placing another Rückert poem at the end, also in A♭ Major, and calling it *"Zum Schluß"* (In Closing).

Schumann loved poetry passionately, but as a composer he felt free to re-shape and re-word the poems he used. In this case he turned Rückert's single stanza to three-part song form: A (lines 1–6), B (lines 7–12), A' (lines 1–4 and 12)

Rhythmically, *"Widmung"* is highly original. The stately bass line is surmounted with glittering figurations in the piano part. The lively tempo must be kept under control to allow clarity in the dotted-eighth rhythm that occurs in most measures, as well as the mordent in measure 4. A *ritardando* prepares for the change of key at measure 14, but the tempo resumes immediately. (After a *ritardando* Schumann usually does not mark the *a tempo* clearly.) The two changes of key signature both produce magical changes of color in the piano part, and in each case the voice supplies the common tone that connects the two keys.

The piano postlude introduces a new and expressive melodic phrase that strongly resembles the opening melody of Schubert's *Ave Maria*. This is not an accident, but symbolizes a prayer of love and thanksgiving.

Sources

Text: *Liebesfrühling*, 1823. This version: *Werke*, vol. I, edited by G. Ellinger. Leipzig: Bibliographisches Institut, 1897.

Music: *Myrthen*, Opus 25, No. 1. Leipzig: Kistner, 1840. Original key: A♭.

Widmung

F. Rückert

Robert Schumann
(Range: B3 – G♭5)

ⓐ "Sincerely, lively." Suggestion: ♩ = ca. 76
ⓑ The inverted mordent is played quickly and before the beat.

Translation: You are my soul, my heart; you are my joy, my pain; you are the world I live in, the heaven I soar in;

ⓒ The appoggiatura is sung quickly and before the beat.

ⓓ Following the ritardando in previous measure, the first tempo resumes here; that is, the half note beat is the same although the subdivision is now in triplets.

ⓔ The turn consists of four equal sixteenths on the second half of beat 2.

oh, you are the grave into which I have sunk all my cares! You are rest and peace; you are the heaven that has been granted to me.

ⓕ The first tempo resumes, but the dynamic is piano.

ⓖ The ritardando continues, still at a piano dynamic, until the tempo resumes in m30 with a forte dynamic. Notice the delicate anticipation of the tonic bass note on beat 3 of m29 ahead of the tonic chord.

Your love gives me worth in my own eyes; the light of your eyes transfigures me. By loving me you lift me above myself. You are my good spirit, my better self.

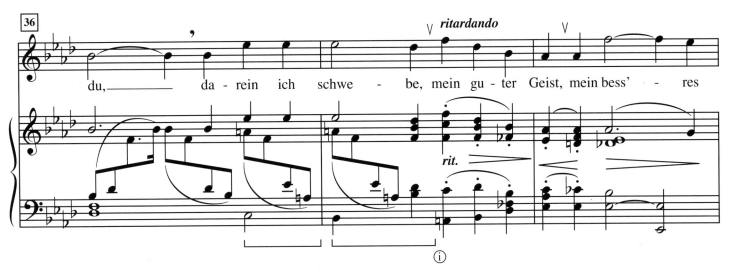

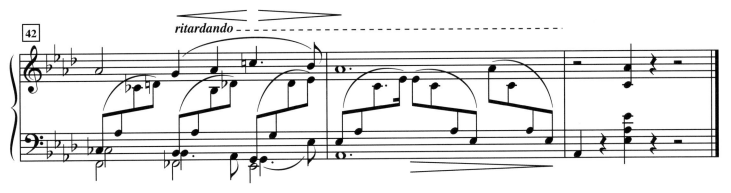

ⓗ "Climbing and hurrying," or *crescendo e stringendo*, continuing through m36.

ⓘ A clean break, lifting the pedal, is necessary before the chord under *mein*. The *ritardando* continues through m38; the tempo resumes in m39.

Der Nussbaum
The Nut Tree

Robert Schumann (1810–1856)

ɛs   gryːnət aen nʊsbaom foːr   dem haos
1. **Es   grünet ein Nussbaum vor   dem Haus,**
There grows   a   nut-tree before the house;

dʊftɪç
2. **Duftig,**
fragrantly,

lʊftɪç
3. **Luftig,**
airily

braetət er blɛtrɪç diː ɛstə   aos
4. **Breitet er blättrig die Äste   aus.**
spreads it leafily the branches out.

fiːl liːplɪçə blyːtən ʃteːən dran
5. **Viel liebliche Blüten   stehen d'ran;**
Many lovely   blossoms are   thereon;

lɪndə
6. **Linde**
gentle

vɪndə
7. **Winde**
winds

kɔmmən ziː hɛrtslɪç tsu: ʔʊmfɑːn
8. **Kommen, sie herzlich zu umfahn.**
come,   them kindly to embrace.

ɛs   flystərn jeː tsvae tsu: tsvae gəpɑːrt
9. **Es   flüstern je zwei zu zwei gepaart,**
There whisper each two by two paired,

naegənt
10. **Neigend,**
inclining,

bɔøgənt
11. **Beugend**
bowing

tsiːrlɪç tsʊm kʊsə diː hɔøptçən tsart
12. **Zierlich zum Kusse die Häuptchen zart.**
daintily to kiss   the little-heads delicate.

ziː flystərn fɔn aenəm mɛːktlaen das
13. **Sie flüstern von einem Mägdlein, das**
They whisper of   a   girl   who

dɛçtə
14. **Dächte**
thought

diː nɛçtə
15. **Die Nächte**
the nights

ʊnt taːgə laŋ vʏstə ax zɛlbər nɪçt vas
16. **Und Tage lang, wüßte, ach! selber nicht was.**
and days long, knew, alas, herself not   something.

ziː flystərn veːr maːk fɛrʃteːn zoː gɑːr
17. **Sie flüstern, — wer mag verstehn so gar**
They whisper (who may understand so very

laezə
18. **Leise**
soft

vaez
19. **Weis'?**
tunes?),

flystərn fɔn brɔøtgam ʊnt nɛçstəm jaːr
20. **Flüstern von Bräut'gam und nächstem Jahr.**
whisper about bridegroom and next   year.

das mɛːktlaen hɔrçət ɛs raoʃt ɪm baom
21. **Das Mägdlein horchet, es   rauscht im Baum;**
The girl   listens; there is-rustling in-the tree.

zeːnənt
22. **Sehnend,**
Longing,

vɛːnənt
23. **Wähnend**
fantasizing,

zɪŋkt ɛs lɛçəlnt ɪn ʃlaːf ʊnt traom
24. **Sinkt es lächelnd in Schlaf und Traum.**
sinks she, smiling, into sleep and dream.

Julius Mosen (1803–1867)
[juːliʊs moozən]

Poetic Background

"How innocent are the dreams of a young girl who falls asleep imagining her future bridegroom."

Mosen's sweetly picturesque poem has a unique form: in each of six four-line stanzas, two long lines enclose two short lines. In every case the two short lines consist of rhyming two-syllable words. Although the effort of maintaining such a strict form results in some awkward grammar, the poem is beautiful when read aloud. The rhyming short lines create hesitations that suggest the swaying of the tree in the breeze.

Title: The variety of tree is not clear. A walnut tree has compound leaves that wave gracefully; a chestnut has more beautiful blossoms.

Line 4: *die Äste* is correct, but some editions preserve an error that Schumann made by writing *die Blätter* (the leaves) instead. Mosen wrote that the tree "spreads its leafy branches out," not "spreads its leafy leaves out."

Line 8: *umfahn* is an archaic form of *umfangen* (encircle, caress).

Lines 14–16: Mosen wrote:

> *Dächte*
> *Nächte*
> *Tagelang, wüßte ach! selber nicht was.*

Schumann changed several words but without altering the meaning significantly. *Dächte* is a subjunctive form: "She would have thought. . ." *Wüßte* is also subjunctive: "She herself would not know. . ." Schumann changed it to *wußte*, probably by accident.

Line 19: *Weis'* is shortened by Schumann, spoiling Mosen's rhyme *leise/Weise*.

Line 20: *von Bräut'gam* lacks its normal article: *von einem Bräutigam*. Some editions have *vom*, but that might imply a definite person rather than a dream figure.

Line 24: *es* is the girl; *Mädchen* is neuter and takes either a neuter or a feminine pronoun.

Musical Background

Clara was nine years and three months younger than Robert Schumann. In this poem he must have identified Clara with the young girl dreaming of future love. This song, composed in February, 1840, is the third in *Myrthen* (for more information see the commentary on *"Widmung"* on page 85). Later songs in *Myrthen* concern a bride and a young mother, roles in which Robert also liked to imagine Clara.

Thinking as a pianist, Schumann often put his first melodic inspiration into the piano part and then invented a vocal melody to match it; that is clearly the case here. The principal melody drifts back and forth between the voice and the piano. Often the voice and piano have the melody at the same time, but slightly out of phase, as in measures 51–55 of this song. Such passages may be difficult to sing accurately and to memorize, but their complexity reflects Schumann's musical personality.

The singer's task is subtle here: to narrate and describe affectionately, as if in remembering what it was like to be such an innocent child/dreamer. By reciting the poem out loud the singer can learn how to bring out the poet's rhyming word-play without losing the smooth legato that Schumann evidently desired.

Sources
Text: *Gedichte*. Leipzig: 1836.
Music: *Myrthen*, Opus 25, no. 3. Leipzig: Kistner, 1840.
Original key: G.

Der Nussbaum

J. Mosen

Robert Schumann
(Range: D4 – F♯5)

ⓐ Suggestion: ♩· = ca. 54

ⓑ Schumann did not say when or how to use the pedal, but he reminded pianists to use it. Earlier pianists used the damper pedal only occasionally, but during Schumann's career pedal use became habitual.

Translation: A walnut tree is turning green in front of the house, spreading out fragrant, airy

blätt - rig die Äs - te aus.

Viel

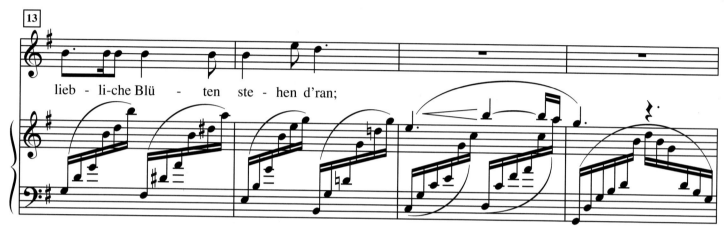

lieb - li-che Blü - ten ste - hen d'ran;

lin - de Win - de kom - men, sie herz - lich zu um - fahn.

Es flü - stern je zwei zu zwei ge-paart,

branches. It has a lot of lovely blossoms; gentle breezes come to caress them. Two by two they whisper,

nei - gend, beu - gend zier - lich zum

Kus - se die Häupt - chen zart.

ritenuto Ⓒ

p

Sie

flü - stern von ei - nem Mägd - lein, das däch - te die

Näch - te und Ta - ge lang,

Ⓒ The ritenuto applies only to the second half of the measure 31; measure 32 is *a tempo*.

bowing and bending delicately to kiss each other. They are whispering about a girl who would be thinking night and day,

wüss - te, ach! sel - ber nicht was.

Sie

flü - stern,   sie flü - stern,   wer

mag ver-steh'n so gar lei - se Weis'?

flü - stern von Bräut' - gam und näch - stem

ⓓ The ritardandos in measures 39 and 49 are less than a measure long; in each case the following measure is *a tempo.*

she herself would not know what about. They are whispering (who could make out such a quiet song?) about a bride-groom and about next

ⓔ The ritardando lasts through measure 56. Lift the pedal before going on to the *a tempo* in measure 57.

year. The girl listens to the rustling of the tree. Longing, imagining, she smiles as she falls asleep and dreams.

Die Lotosblume
The Lotus

Robert Schumann (1810–1856)

di: lo:tɔsblu:mə ɛŋstɪçt
1. Die Lotosblume   ängstigt
The lotus-flower   is-afraid

zɪç   fo:r   der zɔnnə praxt
2. Sich vor   der Sonne Pracht,
(-)   before the sun's   splendor,

ʊnt mɪt gəzɛŋktəm hɑopta
3. Und mit gesenktem Haupte
and   with lowered   head

ɛrvartət zi: trɔəmənt di: naxt
4. Erwartet sie träumend die Nacht.
awaits   she, dreaming, the night.

der mo:nt der ɪst i:r bu:lə
5. Der Mond, der ist ihr Buhle,
the moon, he is   her lover,

er vɛkt zi: mɪt zaenəm lɪçt
6. Er weckt sie mit seinem Licht,
he wakes her with his   light,

ʊnt i:m   ɛntʃlaeərt zi: frɔəntlɪç
7. Und ihm   entschleiert sie freundlich
and to-him unveils   she, friendly,

i:r frɔmməs blu:məngəzɪçt
8. Ihr frommes Blumengesicht.
her worshipful flower-face.

zi: bly:t ʊnt gly:t ʊnt lɔəçtət
9. Sie blüht und glüht und leuchtet,
She blooms and glows and shines

ʊnt ʃtarət ʃtʊm ɪn di: hø:
10. Und starret stumm in   die Höh';
and   stares   silently into the heights;

zi: dʊftət   ʊnt vaenət ʊnt tsɪtərt
11. Sie duftet   und weinet und zittert
she perfumes and weeps and trembles

fo:r li:bə ʊnt li:bəsve:
12. Vor Liebe und Liebesweh'.
for love and love's-pain.

Heinrich Heine (1797–1856)

Poetic Background

"She is a tender flower, who responds only to love that is quiet and gentle."

The sacred lotus, often seen in Hindu and Buddhist art, grows in water and sends up a large pink or white flower on a single stalk.

Heine read a Sanskrit play, *Sakontala*, by Kalidasa (5th century), translated into German by H. G. Forster in 1791. Forster's explanatory notes about the play contain this passage about the lotus: ". . . it is the flower of the night, 'the cooling flower, that is afraid when the day appears, that is afraid of the stars,' that only opens up to the moon, gives its fragrance only to the moon, and lowers its head before the rays of the sun." Heine transformed this passage into a poem of three stanzas.

This poem, written sometime in 1822, is closely related to another Heine poem, *"Auf Flügeln des Gesanges,"* which is the text of a song by Mendelssohn. The commentary to that song, found on page 75, tells more about Heine's interest in India and about his peculiar way of imagining that certain people resembled certain flowers and plants. It also tells about his collection of poems called *Lyrical Intermezzo*, in which this is the tenth poem.

Lines 1–2: *ängstigt sich* is a verb with its reflexive pronoun, which must always be in close proximity. An actor would never think of pausing between the two words. Because of the odd fact that Schumann imposed a rest after *ängstigt*, the singer must create, by any possible means, a psychological link between the first two phrases.

Line 5: The first edition of the poem has *"Der Mond, das ist. . ."* but later editions use the more normal grammar. *Buhle* is an archaic word for "lover," usually an extramarital lover.

Musical Background

Composed in February, 1840, this is another song that was included in *Myrthen*, Robert's wedding gift to Clara. (Please read more about *Myrthen* on page 85.) In this poem the shy flower obviously symbolizes a young woman and the moon her gentle lover. Eric Sams says, "The sheer depths of devotion revealed in this song are almost frightening. The idea of the unveiled bride is the secret source of the music."

A three stanza poem like this is often set to music in a three-part form (ABA), but Schumann avoids the obvious and gives each stanza new music. The first ends on the dominant of the main key (m9). Using a modulation with the common tone in the voice, the second stanza begins in the key of the lowered sixth, and it moves to the tonic key without reaching a perfect cadence. The deceptive cadence in m17 gives the third stanza an ambiguous beginning. After a long detour to the subdominant key, the voice finally reaches a tonic cadence in m25. Even then the tonic note is not in the bass until the final resolution in m27. The long delay in reaching the tonic clearly symbolizes the "pain of love."

Notice that the vocal melody is sometimes doubled by inner chord tones in the piano. In m25 the piano echoes what the singer sang in the previous measure although the notation obscures the fact.

Sources

Text: *Tragödien, nebst einem lyrischen Intermezzo.* Berlin, 1823. *Lyrisches Intermezzo* was also a section of *Buch der Lieder*, 1827. This version: *Heine Säkularausgabe, Gedichte, 1812–1827*, vol. 1., Berlin: Akademie-Verlag, 1979.

Music: *Myrthen*, Opus 25, no. 7. Leipzig: Kistner, 1840. Original key: F.

Die Lotosblume

H. Heine

Robert Schumann
(Range: C4 – G5)

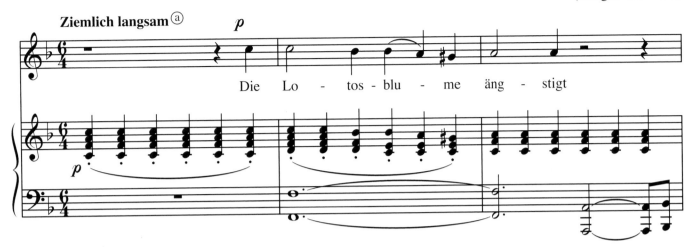

Die Lo - tos-blu - me äng - stigt

sich vor der Son - ne Pracht,   und mit ge - senk - tem Haup - te   er -

war - tet sie träu-mend die Nacht.   Der Mond der ist— ihr Buh - le,   er

ⓐ "Rather slowly." Suggestion: ♩ = ca. 104

Translation: The lotus flower is afraid of the sun's magnificence; she bows her head and waits dreamily for the night to come. The moon is her favorite lover; his

ⓑ "Little by little faster." The *accelerando* continues to m23.

light wakens her, and she gladly reveals her worshipful flower face. She blooms and glows and gleams and gazes silently upward; she gives off fragrance, weeps, and trembles from love and the pain of love.

In der Fremde, Opus 39:1

[ɪn der frɛmdə]

In a Foreign Land

Robert Schumann (1810–1856)

ɑos   der hɑemɑːt   hɪntər den blɪtsən   roːt
1. **Aus   der Heimat   hinter den Blitzen   rot,**
From the homeland behind the lightning red,

dɑː   kɔmmən di vɔlkən   heːr
2. **Da   kommen die Wolken her.**
there come   the clouds   this-way.

ɑːbər fɑːtər ʊnt mʊtər zɪnt laŋə toːt
3. **Aber Vater und Mutter sind lange tot,**
But   Father and Mother are   long   dead;

ɛs   kɛnt   mɪç   dɔrt kɑenər meːr
4. **Es   kennt mich dort keiner   mehr.**
there knows me   there nobody anymore.

viː   balt ax viː   balt kɔmt   di ʃtɪllə tsaet
5. **Wie bald, ach wie bald kommt die stille Zeit,**
How soon, ah how soon comes the quiet time,

dɑː   ruːə ɪç ɑox ʊnt yːbər miːr
6. **Da   ruhe ich auch, und über mir**
then rest I   also, and over   me

rɑoʃt   di ʃøːnə   vɑlt ʔaenzamkaet
7. **Rauscht die schöne   Waldeinsamkeit,**
rustles   the beautiful forest-solitude,

ʊnt kɑenər kɛnt   mɪç meːr   hiːr
8. **Und keiner kennt mich mehr   hier.**
and nobody knows me   anymore here.

Joseph von Eichendorff (1788–1857)

Poetic Background

"I shall die here, far from home, and no one will miss me."

Eichendorff first used this poem in a short novel called *Viel Lärmen um Nichts,* which is also the German title of Shakespeare's *Much Ado about Nothing.* In a rather enigmatic scene a beautiful young woman sings this poem with guitar accompaniment, but there is no clear explanation of what it means.

Line 1: *den Blitzen rot* instead of *den roten Blitzen* is a word order that comes from folk songs. The image combines a red sunset with lightning, perhaps visible among far away clouds. Looking to the west, the singer thinks of the homeland that lies in that direction, even farther away than the clouds.

Line 4: *Es* takes the place of the real subject of the sentence, *keiner,* which comes after the verb instead of in its normal position. *Dort* refers to the homeland.

Line 5: *ach* was added by Schumann. Beginning here, the present tense verbs all refer to the near future, as in the English sentence: "Tomorrow I'm going away."

Line 7: *rauscht* is Eichendorff's favorite word for natural sounds. *Waldeinsamkeit* is a famous example of an invented compound word, carrying the idea that solitude in the forest is different from elsewhere. The image is beautiful even though solitude cannot literally *rauschen.* The singer expects to be buried in a forest, like an animal, rather than in a cemetery.

Line 8: *keiner. . .* was written by Eichendorff as: *keiner mehr kennt mich auch hier.*

Musical Background

Schumann's *Liederkreis,* Opus 39 (Song Cycle), settings of 12 poems by Eichendorff, opens with this melancholy song. The "cycle" does not tell any story, but Schumann scholars have found in it a number of musical symbols like encoded messages to Clara. Schumann's mind was very much on marriage when he composed these songs, and it is possible that he was even imagining Clara's singing voice.

The mention of a guitar in Eichendorff's novel may have suggested using a broken chord accompaniment for the whole song. Simple in appearance, the song is perfectly shaped, exquisitely colored. In m22 and m24 Neapolitan harmony is used over a pedal point.

"In der Fremde" was written in May, 1840, but its publication was delayed. A group of 12 Eichendorff settings was published in 1842, entitled *Liederkreis* (Song Cycle). The first song in the group was *"Der frohe Wandersmann"* (The Happy Wanderer), but when the cycle was revised in 1850, *"In der Fremde"* was put in its place. The eighth song in the cycle is also called *"In der Fremde,"* but it has a different poem.

Oddly, the surviving manuscript of *"In der Fremde"* is in Clara's handwriting rather than Robert's, but no one seriously doubts that this is his composition.

The first complete performance of Opus 39 was sung by baritone Julius Stockhausen.

Sources

Text: *Viel Lärmen um Nichts,* 1832. This version: *Werke.* München: Winkler-Verlag, 1970.

Music: *Liederkreis* (revised version), Opus 39, no.1. Leipzig: Whistling, 1850. Original key: F♯ minor.

In der Fremde

J. von Eichendorff

Robert Schumann
(Range: F♯4 – E5)

ⓐ "Not fast." Suggestion: ♩ = ca. 66
ⓑ Sing the double grace notes before the beat.

Translation: From my homeland, which is hidden by red lightning, clouds are coming this way. But Father and Mother died long ago and nobody knows me there anymore. How soon, very soon,

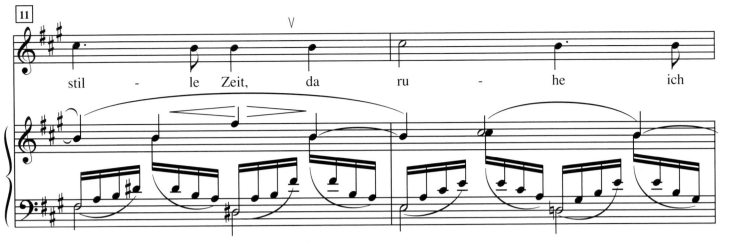

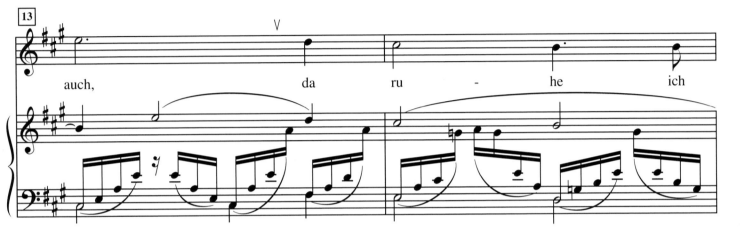

that quiet time will come when I shall rest too, and the solitude of the forest will surround me,

schö - ne Wald - ein - sam - keit,   und

kei - ner kennt mich mehr hier,   und

kei - ner kennt mich mehr hier.

and no one will know me here anymore.

Ein Jüngling liebt ein Mädchen
A Fellow Loves a Girl

Robert Schumann (1810–1856)

aen jʏŋlɪŋ liːpt aen mɛːtçən
1. Ein Jüngling liebt ein Mädchen,
A   youth   loves a   girl,

diː hat aenən ʔandərn ɛrvɛːlt
2. Die hat einen Andern erwählt;
who has an   other-one chosen;

der ʔandrə liːpt aenə ʔandrə
3. Der And're   liebt eine And're,
the other-youth loves an   other-girl,

ʊnt hat zɪç   mɪt diːzər fɛrmɛːlt
4. Und hat sich   mit dieser   vermählt.
and has himself with the-latter married

das mɛːtçən nɪmt aos ʔɛrgər
5. Das Mädchen nimmt aus   Ärger
The girl   takes, out-of annoyance,

den ʔeːrstən bɛstən man
6. Den ersten   besten Mann,
the first,   best   man

der ʔiːr ɪn den veːk gəlaofən
7. Der ihr in den Weg gelaufen;
who her into the way has-run;

der jʏŋlɪŋ   ɪst yːbəl dran
8. Der Jüngling ist übel dran.
the youth   is badly on-it.

ɛs ɪst aenə ʔaltə gəʃɪçtə
9. Es ist eine alte   Geschichte,
It is an   old   story,

dɔx blaept ziː ɪmmər nɔø
10. Doch bleibt sie immer neu;
yet stays it always new,

ʊnt vem   ziː jʊst pasiːrət
11. Und wem   sie just passieret,
and to-whom it just happened,

deːm brɪçt das hɛrts ɛntsvae
12. Dem bricht das Herz entzwei.
him breaks the heart in-two.

Heinrich Heine (1797–1856)

Poetic Background

"When a man sees his beloved marry the wrong man, it may be a joke to other people but it means heartbreak to him."

When Heine was twenty, a wealthy uncle set him up in business as manager of a textile shop. Heine had no interest in textiles, but he wanted to impress his cousin Amalie, his uncle's pretty, smug and capricious daughter. The shop failed, and worse, Amalie didn't care about the poems Heine wrote for her. When he went away to study law, he thought that Amalie would wait for him. Two years later she married a wealthy land owner. Heine thought that he had been betrayed, that his angel had turned out to be a devil in disguise. His anger toward Amalie supplied the impulse to write hundreds of poems about betrayed love.

Heine was impressed by the folksong-like verses of Robert Burns and of Wilhelm Müller, who wrote the poems of Schubert's *Die schöne Müllerin* and *Die Winterreise*. Both poets typically used a conventional ballad stanza: four short lines, with a simple rhyme scheme. Heine adopted this form and added his own element, a cynical twist at the end, even in the final line, as in this poem.

This poem is the 39th in the collection called *Lyrical Intermezzo* (described on page 75).

Line 1: *Mädchen*, Heine wrote *Mägdlein* in the first edition, but later editions have *Mädchen*.

Line 5: *nimmt* is Schumann's word choice; Heine wrote *heiratet* (marries).

Line 7: *ihr in den Weg* uses dative case where English uses possessive: "into her way." Heine omits the auxiliary verb *ist*, but it is understood: *ist gelaufen* (has run).

Line 12: *dem bricht das Herz* again uses dative in place of possessive: "his heart breaks."

Musical Background

In May, 1840, immediately after completing the Eichendorff *Liederkreis*, even on the same sheet of paper, Schumann began to compose *Dichterliebe* (Poet's Love). He chose texts from among the 65 poems in *Lyrisches Intermezzo* and put them into an order that suggests a story of love, betrayal and resignation.

Of the 16 songs in *Dichterliebe*, the first six recall an idealistic love that borders on worship of the young woman. The seventh song, with its ironic text, "I'll not complain. . . ," announces the betrayal, followed by several songs that mingle grief and anger. In the eleventh song, *"Ein Jüngling. . . ,"* the poet tries to deal with his disappointment by mocking it and himself. Here, the singer is a story-teller; in the last phrase he lets us know that the story is his own. Even so, the piano postlude resumes the carefree mood of the opening.

Schumann originally dedicated the cycle to his close friend Felix Mendelssohn, but changed the dedication to honor a great soprano, Wilhelmine Schröder-Devrient, who had won early fame as the first Leonora in Beethoven's *Fidelio*. The first complete public performances of *Dichterliebe* were sung by baritone Julius Stockhausen with Johannes Brahms at the piano (1861) and with Clara Schumann at the piano (1862).

Sources

Text: *Zwei Tragödien nebst einem lyrischen Intermezzo.* Berlin, 1823. This version: *Heine Säkularausgabe, Gedichte, 1812–1827*, vol. 1. Berlin: Akademie-Verlag, 1979.

Music: *Dichterliebe*, Opus 48, no. 11. Leipzig: Peters, 1844. Original key: E♭.

Ein Jüngling liebt ein Mädchen

H. Heine

Robert Schumann
(Range: B♭3 – F5)

Ein Jüng-ling liebt ein Mäd - chen, die hat ei-nen An-dern er-wählt; der An-d're liebt ei-ne An - d're, und hat sich mit die-ser ver-mählt. Das Mäd - chen nimmt aus Är - ger den er-sten, be-sten Mann, der ihr in den Weg ge-

ⓐ There is no tempo marking. Suggestion: ♩ = ca. 96

Translation: A fellow loves a girl, who has already picked out another man; that man falls in love with another girl and marries her. Just for spite the first girl picks up the first available man;

ⓑ Most interpreters assume that there is an *a tempo* in m24.

that's bad news for the fellow who loved her to start with. It's an old story, but also new at the same time, and when it happens to a man, it breaks his heart in two.

Du Ring an meinem Finger
You Ring on My Finger

Robert Schumann (1810–1856)

duː rɪŋ   an maenəm fɪŋər
1. Du Ring an meinem Finger,
You ring on my   finger,

maen gɔldənəs rɪŋəlaen
2. Mein goldenes Ringelein,
my   golden   little-ring,

ɪç drʏkə dɪç frɔm   ʔan diː lɪppən
3. Ich drücke dich fromm an die Lippen,
I   press you devoutly to   my lips,

dɪç frɔm   ʔan das hɛrtsə maen
4. Dich fromm an das Herze mein.
you devoutly to   the heart mine.

ɪç hat iːn ʔaosgətrɔømət
5. Ich hatt' ihn ausgeträumet,
I   had it   dreamed-out,

der kɪnthaet   friːtlɪçən ʃøːnən traom
6. Der Kindheit   friedlich schönen Traum,
the childhood's peacefully beautiful dream;

ɪç fant ʔallaen mɪç   fɛrloːrən
7. Ich fand allein   mich   verloren
I   found alone   myself lost

ɪm ʔøːdən ʔunʔɛntlɪçən raom
8. Im öden   unendlichen Raum.
in barren unending   space.

9. Du Ring an meinem Finger,

daː hast duː mɪç eːrst bəleːrt
10. Da   hast du mich erst belehrt,
there have you me   first instructed,

hast maenəm blɪk ʔɛrʃlɔsən
11. Hast meinem Blick erschlossen
have to-my   gaze opened

dɛs leːbəns unʔɛntlɪçən tiːfən veːrt
12. Des Lebens unendlichen, tiefen Wert.
[the] life's   unending,   deep value.

ɪç veːrt ʔiːm diːnən iːm   leːbən
13. Ich werd' ihm dienen, ihm   leben,
I   will   him serve, for-him live,

iːm   ʔangəhøːrən gants
14. Ihm   angehören   ganz,
to-him belong   entirely,

hɪn zɛlbər mɪç geːbən unt fɪndən
15. Hin selber mich geben und finden
away self   me   to-give and to-find

fɛrkleːrt mɪç ɪn zaenəm gants
16. Verklärt   mich in seinem Glanz.
transfigured me in his   radiance.

17. Du Ring an meinem Finger,
18. Mein goldenes Ringelein,
19. Ich drücke dich fromm an die Lippen,
20. Dich fromm an das Herze mein.

Adalbert von Chamisso (1781–1838)
[aːdalbɛrt fɔn ʃamɪso]

Poetic Background
"My dear wedding ring shows me the whole future direction of my life."

Chamisso wrote a sequence of nine poems entitled *Frauen-Liebe und Leben* (Woman's Life and Love), that records the emotions of a woman from the first sight of the man she loves through courtship, marriage and child-rearing to widowhood. She finds the value of her life in love for her husband and her baby girl.

Chamisso's 1830 poems are open to criticism as being a man's view of what a woman ought to be, but they doubtlessly express the ideals of middle class German life at that time. The marriage of Robert and Clara Schumann is an example of this ideal: her first responsibility was the care of him and her children. Her life as a musician, while remarkably productive, was nevertheless secondary.

Schumann did not use the ninth poem, in which the woman blesses her granddaughter and exhorts her to live as she has done, for love.

Title: *Frauen-Liebe und Leben* is Chamisso's punctuation of the title, a shortened form of *Frauenliebe und Frauenleben.* (Some editors write *Frauenliebe*, and some use a hyphen before *-Leben*.) The poem and song are numbered "4" but have no titles.

Line 5: *ihn* refers to *Traum* in the next line.

Line 6: *friedlich schönen* is Schumann's version where Chamisso wrote only *friedlichen*.

Lines 7–8: *ich fand . . . Raum*, feeling herself finished with childhood, she faces a future that seems empty and endless unless her destiny is fulfilled in marriage.

Lines 8 and 12: *unendlichen* is often mispronounced; there is no [t] after *un-*.

Line 12: *tiefen* is also added by Schumann.

Line 13: *werd'* is Chamisso's word, a future tense. Schumann wrote *"Ich will ihm dienen,"* which implies conscious intention. The change, possibly unintentional and not an improvement, should not be kept.

Line 15: *geben und finden* are both in future tense, governed by *werd'*.

Lines 15–16: *finden . . . Glanz*: the complete clause in normal word order would be *ich werde mich in seinem Glanz verklärt finden. Verklärt* means transformed in outward appearance, also exalted or glorified. She speaks metaphorically of her bridegroom as if he radiates light that will also brighten her image.

Musical Background
In 1827 Carl Loewe had published his settings of Chamisso's *Frauenliebe.* Schumann probably knew this fact but could not resist composing these songs that exactly mirrored the love that

his dear Clara had for him. In June 1840 Robert and Clara were in court with a lawsuit against Clara's father, Friedrich Wieck, fighting for their right to marry. Wieck accused Robert of habitual drunkenness, but he produced no evidence. On July 7 the court ruled in the couple's favor; exhilarated, Robert wrote the music of *Frauenliebe* in two days, July 11 and 12.

Pure happiness glows through this song that the bride sings to her golden ring. The hymnlike phrasing poses a technical problem; the singer must renew her breath repeatedly without delaying the even flow of eighth notes in the accompaniment. Except in measures 25–32 the piano part is contrapuntal throughout, but the moving voices are low and easily sound muddy. Careful fingering and pedalling are needed to avoid an unwelcome thickness in the accompaniment.

The first complete performance of Opus 42 was sung by baritone Julius Stockhausen, although no male singers have performed it in more recent times.

Sources

Text: *Gedichte.* Leipzig: Weidmann, second edition, 1834.
Music: *Frauen-Liebe und Leben*, Opus 42, No. 4. Leipzig: Whistling, 1843. Original key: E♭.

Du Ring an meinem Finger

A. von Chamisso

Robert Schumann
(Range: C4 – F5)

ⓐ "Sincerely." Suggestion: ♩ = ca. 56

Translation: You ring on my finger, my little gold ring, I press you devotedly to my lips, to my heart. I

had finished with childhood's peaceful dream; I found myself alone, facing a barren and unending future. You ring on my finger, then you taught me for the first time

21 mei - nem Blick er - schlos - sen des_ Le - bens un - end - li - chen,

24 **Nach und nach rascher.** ⓑ tie - fen Wert. Ich werd' ihm die - nen, ihm le - ben, ihm

27 *ritardando* an - ge - hö - ren ganz, hin sel - ber mich ge - ben und

30 *ritardando* fin - den ver - klärt mich, und fin - den ver - klärt mich in sei - nem Glanz. Du_

ⓑ "Gradually faster." The accelerando lasts through measures 27. The ritardando in measure 28 reduces the tempo (29–30). The second ritardando reduces it even more, and the first tempo returns at measure 33.

and opened my eyes to life's deep, infinite worth. I will serve him, live for him, belong entirely to him, give myself to him and find myself illuminated in his light.

Ring   an mei - nem   Fin   -   ger,   mein.   gol - de - nes Rin   -   ge -

lein,   ich__ drü - cke dich fromm an die   Lip   -   pen,   dich

fromm   an die Lip-pen, an das   Her   -   ze mein!

ⓒ Schumann asked to have the damper pedal down from beat 3 until the second half of beat 4. (Obviously, the pedal has been in use throughout the song, but this is a special effect.)

ⓓ Schumann asked to have the damper pedal down through beats 1 and 2, released on beat 3.

Nachtlied
[na̱xtliːt]
Night Song

yːbəɾ ʔallən gɪpfəln
1. **Über allen Gipfeln**
Over all mountain-peaks

ɪst ruː
2. **Ist Ruh',**
is rest;

ɪn ʔallən vɪpfəln
3. **In allen Wipfeln**
in all treetops

ʃpyːrəst duː
4. **Spürest du**
sense you

kɑom a̱enən hɑox
5. **Kaum einen Hauch;**
hardly a breath.

diː føːgəlaen ʃva̱egən ɪm valdə
6. **Die Vögelein schweigen im Walde.**
The little-birds are-silent in-the wood.

va̱rtə nuːr ba̱ldə
7. **Warte nur, balde**
Wait only, soon

ru̱ːəst duː ɑox
8. **Ruhest du auch.**
rest you also.

Johann Wolfgang von Goethe (1749–1832)

Poetic Background

"The peacefulness of Nature reassures me that soon I shall also find peace."

While on a walking trip through mountains in Thuringia, Goethe spent the night of September 7, 1780, in a little frame hunting lodge near Ilmenau. There he wrote these lines in pencil on the wall. A half century later he re-visited the cabin and wept when he saw the words still there. The poem points toward death but in a peaceful and reassuring way.

This was published with another short poem, *"Der du von dem Himmel bist,"* called *"Wandrers Nachtlied"* (Wanderer's Night Song). The heading over this poem was *"Ein Gleiches"* (one of the same), which is not a title at all. Subsequently these two famous little poems were known as *"Wandrers Nachtlied I und II"* or known by their first lines.

The American poet Henry Wadsworth Longfellow made this translation of Goethe's poem:

> *O'er all the hill-tops*
> *Is quiet now,*
> *In all the tree-tops*
> *Hearest thou*
> *Hardly a breath;*
> *The birds are asleep in the trees:*
> *Wait; soon like these*
> *Thou too shalt rest.*

No poem in German literature has been more admired and more exhaustively analyzed than these eight lines containing 24 words. The images in the poem include the mineral (line 1), vegetable (line 3) and animal (line 5) kingdoms, all at rest. When Goethe finally addresses himself, he draws no distinction between himself and the realms of Nature. Goethe's sense of unity with Nature places him philosophically above the lesser poets who saw Nature as if it were an extension of themselves and their human feelings.

Line 3: *Wipfeln*, from the window of the lodge Goethe looked down on a forest of hemlock trees.

Line 6: *Vöglein*, Goethe wrote *"Vögelein."*

Line 7: *balde* is an older form of *bald* and is still in dialect use.

Musical Background

In July 1850 Robert and Clara Schumann still lived in Dresden, but they were planning a move to Düsseldorf in August. His health was not robust, but his depression had not yet caused him to be hospitalized. During July and August he composed 18 songs; only a few, including this one, are considered equal to the great songs of 1840.

"Nachtlied" has no strong resemblance to Schubert's setting of the same poem, published in 1827. But it does resemble Schubert's *"Meeres Stille"* (Sea Calm), D. 216; both songs are in C Major, in common time, and accompanied by heavy chords. But the songs create quite different effects: Schubert describes a becalmed sea that is threatening, even potentially deadly to the crew of a sailing vessel; Schumann describes a comforting calm that promises rest to a weary and troubled traveler.

Schumann's original metronome marking prevents us from taking the song too slowly. The long chords and solemn melodic movement create the impression that the song as a whole is "very slow," but the underlying beat is moderate in speed. The slow triplets in m19 and m21 contribute to the sense of calm by providing a contrast to the prevailing long chords.

There are two other settings of this poem by Franz Liszt, and one each by Schubert (D. 768), Carl Friedrich Zelter, Ferdinand Hiller, Hugo Wolf, Nicolai Medtner, and many others. Charles Ives wrote one entitled *"Ilmenau."*

Sources

Text: *Werke*, vol 1. Berlin: Tempel Verlag, 1959.

Music: *Lieder und Gesänge*, Opus 96, no. 1. Original key: C.

Nachtlied

J. W. von Goethe

Robert Schumann

(Range: D4 – F5)

ⓐ "Very slow." The metronome marking is Schumann's own.

Translation: Over all the mountaintops there is peace; in all the treetops you can hear hardly a breath of wind. The birds are quiet in the woods. Just wait; soon you will rest, too.

Du bist wie eine Blume
You are Like a Flower

Franz Liszt (1811–1886)
[franfs lıst]

du   bıst viː <u>ae</u>nə bl<u>uː</u>mə
1. Du bist wie eine Blume,
You are   like a   flower,

zoː hɔlt   ʊnt ʃøːn   ʊnt raen
2. So hold   und schön   und rein;
so   lovely and beautiful and pure;

ıç   ʃao   dıç an ʊnt v<u>eː</u>muːt
3. Ich schau' dich an, und Wehmut
I   look   you   at, and melancholy

ʃlaeçt   miːr   ıns   hɛrts hın<u>ae</u>n
4. Schleicht mir   in's   Herz hinein.
creeps   to-me into-the heart in.

miːr   ıst als ɔp ıç diː h<u>ɛ</u>ndə
5. Mir   ist, als ob ich die Hände
To-me is   as   if   I   the hands

aofs   haopt diːr l<u>eː</u>gən zɔlt
6. Auf's Haupt dir   legen   sollt',
on-the head your lay   should,

beːtənt das dıç gɔt ɛrh<u>a</u>ltə
7. Betend, dass dich Gott erhalte
praying that you   God   preserve,

zoː raen ʊnt ʃøːn   ʊnt hɔlt
8. So rein und schön   und hold.
so   pure and beautiful and lovely.

Heinrich Heine (1797–1856)

Poetic Background

"When I see your innocent loveliness, I want to pray that you will always remain as you are now."

Various witnesses said that they knew the origin of this poem, but they did not agree on the identity of the young woman described. In August or September, 1822, Heine visited the estate of a friend, Eugen von Breza, near Gnesen, Poland. There he seems to have met and fallen in love with a girl named Mirjam, the daughter of the local rabbi. Details are unclear.

Heine's brother Maximilian, in his *Erinnerungen* (Memories, 1869), wrote about living in the room next to Heinrich's in Lüneburg in the period between May 1823 and January 1824: "Many of his most glorious poems, often with the ink still wet, he read aloud to me, for instance, 'Du bist wie eine Blume'." However, it may be that Maximilian was merely thinking of great poems in general and did not have a specific recollection about *"Du bist wie eine Blume."*

Line 7: *dich Gott,* Heine wrote *Gott dich.*

Musical Background

Liszt was at the peak of his success as a piano virtuoso in 1843, when he wrote *"Du bist wie eine Blume."* Aside from concertizing, especially to raise money for a Beethoven monument, he composed constantly. When not traveling, he lived with Countess Marie d'Agoult, the mother of his three children.

Closely contemporary with Mendelssohn and Schumann, Liszt was more international in his viewpoint and more open to influences from non-German sources. For instance, he greatly admired Hector Berlioz and Frédéric Chopin and was their friend. He made daring experiments in harmony, especially in his later works. Even here, he surprises the listener with a new tone color under the word *"betend,"* a major chord built on the submediant scale tone. Still more surprising is the sudden return of the tonic key at *"erhalte,"* although one has been expecting a cadence in the submediant key.

Compared with earlier composers in this volume, Liszt provides far more detailed instructions about dynamics and even about vocal color, as in *mezza voce* (half voice) and *sotto voce* (under voice, that is, very softly). When a composer gives us so much interpretive help, we have a duty to obey the suggestions.

Vocal *portamentos,* rarely seen in lieder, are notated in m27 and m37.

More than 200 composers have published settings of *"Du bist wie eine Blume,"* according to Philip L. Miller, who lists many of them in *The Ring of Words.* Schumann's is the most famous, but the one by Anton Rubinstein is also very effective.

Sources

Text first published in: *Rheinische Flora,* Feb. 13, 1825. Included in *Reisebilder,* part I (1826), and then in *Buch der Lieder* (1827) as no. 47 in the series *Die Heimkehr* (Return Home). This version: *Heine Säkularausgabe, Gedichte, 1812–1827,* vol. 1. Berlin: Akademie-Verlag, 1979.

Music: *6 Lieder.* Leipzig: Hofmeister, between 1844–5. This version: *Werke,* volume 59. Leipzig: Breitkopf & Härtel. (A note says: first published, 1844, newly arranged, 1860.) For tenor. Original key: A Major.

Du bist wie eine Blume

H. Heine

Franz Liszt
(Range: E4 – G5)

ⓐ "Slowly, most tenderly." Suggestion: ♩ = ca. 80

Translation: You are like a flower, so lovely and beautiful and pure; when I look at you, melancholy feelings come into my heart.

I think that I should lay my hands on your head, praying that God will keep you just this pure and beautiful and lovely.

An die Entfernte

[an diː ɛntfɛrntə]

To the Distant One

Josephine Lang (1815–1880)

[jozefiːnə laŋ]

di:zə roːzə pflʏk ʔɪç hiːr
1. Diese Rose pflück' ich hier
This rose pick I here

ɪn der frɛmdən fɛrnə
2. In der fremden Ferne;
in the foreign distance;

liːbəs hɛrtsə diːr ax diːr
3. Liebes Herze, dir, ach dir
dear heart, to-you, ah, to-you

brɛçt ʔɪç ziː zoː gɛrnə
4. Brächt' ich sie so gerne!
would-break I it so gladly!

dɔx bɪs ɪç tsuː diːr maːk tsiːən
5. Doch bis ich zu dir mag ziehen
Still, until I to you may travel

fiːlə vaetə maelən
6. Viele weite Meilen,
many long miles,

ɪst diː roːzə lɛŋst dahɪn
7. Ist die Rose längst dahin,
is the rose long gone-away,

dɛn diː roːzən ʔaelən
8. Denn die Rosen eilen.
for the roses hurry.

niː zɔl vaetər zɪç ɪns lant
9. Nie soll weiter sich in's Land
Never should farther itself into-the land

liːp fɔn liːbə vaːgən
10. Lieb' von Liebe wagen,
love from love dare [to go]

als zɪç blyːənt ɪn der hant
11. Als sich blühend in der Hand
than itself, blooming, in the hand

lɛst diː roːzə traːgən
12. Läßt die Rose tragen;
lets the rose be-carried;

oːdər als diː naxtigal
13. Oder als die Nachtigall
or than the nightingale

halmə brɪŋt tsʊm nɛstə
14. Halme bringt zum Neste,
straws brings to-the nest

oːdər als iːr zyːsər ʃal
15. Oder als ihr süßer Schall
or than its sweet sound

vandərt mɪt dem vɛstə
16. Wandert mit dem Weste.
travels with the west-wind.

Nikolaus Lenau (1802–1850)

Poetic Background

"I am thinking of you from far away and regretting that we are so far apart."

The light-hearted spirit of this poem is an exception to the predominantly gloomy tone of Lenau's work.

Line 3: *Herze,* Lenau wrote *Mädchen* (girl). Lang's word choice avoids gender.

Line 5: *ziehen,* Lenau wrote *ziehn* (in one syllable), forming a better rhyme with *dahin* in line 7.

Musical Background

Lang's forebears included several professional sopranos and an opera conductor; her husband was an amateur poet. With this background her compositional talent naturally developed toward writing lieder. *"An die Entfernte"* is chosen to represent her here because the simple charm of her melody perfectly matches that of Lenau's poem. Exploring her other songs, a singer will find that many of them possess greater depth and harmonic complexity than this one.

Lang turned Lenau's four short stanzas into two longer, nearly identical ones, but she took care to vary the dynamic markings. Some points of interest are the *stringendo* in m19, a rare marking in vocal music, and the charming extension of the last phrase in mm 42–44. The piano postlude introduces a vigorous new theme that brings the song to a happy conclusion, perhaps with the thought of seeing the beloved again in the near future.

Sources

Text: *"An die Entfernte"* (comprising two short poems written in 1838, of which this is the first, *"I."*), in a larger group of poems, *Liebesklänge* (Love's Melodies). This version: *Sämtliche Werke,* Leipzig: Hesse & Becker, 1900.

Music: *Sechs Lieder,* Opus 13, no. 5, Mainz: B. Schott's Söhne (between 1844–51). This version: Leipzig: Breitkopf & Härtel, 1883, reprinted in *Selected Songs,* ed. Judith Tick. New York: Da Capo Press, 1982. Original key: F.

An die Entfernte

Nikolaus Lenau

Josephine Lang
(Range: C4 – F5)

Die - se Ro - se pflück' ich hier   in der frem-den Fer - ne;   lie - bes Her-ze,

dir, ach dir brächt' ich sie so ger - ne! Doch bis ich zu dir mag zie-hen

ⓐ Suggestion: ♩ = ca. 84
ⓑ Lang placed a long slur over mm 5–8 to indicate legato singing for the whole song.

Translation: I am picking a rose here far from home; dear one, how I would love to be picking it for you!
But if I could travel

ⓒ Lang did not say how long the *stringendo* should last. *Tempo primo* might return in measure 21, simultaneously with the *piano* marking in the accompaniment, or at the end of measure 22, where the music of the introduction returns.

the many miles to you, the rose would be wilted, for roses have a short life. Lovers should never travel farther away from each other than a blooming rose can be carried by hand,

or farther than a nightingale carries straws to build a nest, or farther than the nightingale's sweet song can be carried on the west wind.

Aus meinen großen Schmerzen
From My Great Pains

Robert Franz (1815–1892)
[ˈroːbɛrt frants]

ɑos   maenən   groːsən   ʃmɛrtsən
1. **Aus**   **meinen**   **großen**   **Schmerzen**
   From   my   great   pains

max   ɪc   diː   klaenən   liːdər
2. **Mach' ich die kleinen Lieder;**
   make   I   the   little   songs;

diː   heːbən   iːr   klɪŋənt   gəfiːdər
3. **Die heben ihr klingend Gefieder**
   they   lift   their   ringing   plumage

ʊnt   flatərn   nax   iːrəm   hɛrtsən
4. **Und flattern nach ihrem Herzen.**
   and   flutter   toward   her   heart.

ziː   fandən   den   veːk   tsuːr   trɑotən
5. **Sie fanden den Weg zur Trauten,**
   They   found   the   way   to-the   dear-one,

dɔx   kɔmmən   ziː   viːdər   ʊnt   klɑːgən
6. **Doch kommen sie wieder und klagen,**
   but   come   they   again   and   wail,

ʊnt   klɑːgən   ʊnt   vɔllən   nɪçt   zɑːgən
7. **Und klagen, und wollen nicht sagen,**
   and   wail   and   will   not   say

vas   ziː   ɪm   hɛrtsən   ʃɑotən
8. **Was sie im Herzen schauten.**
   what   they   in-the heart   saw.

Heinrich Heine (1797–1856)

Poetic Background

"I send thoughts of love to you, but only doubts and suspicions come back to me."

Heine suffered deeply from his feeling that a cousin, who seemed to be in love with him, betrayed him by marrying another man. His anger poured out in literally hundreds of lyric poems that used every imaginable image to tell the world about his hurt feelings.

This poem, like many of Heine's, consists of two four-line stanzas, as do myriads of folk songs. Heine's distinction is in his use of many kinds of irony, in this case, the incongruity between his monstrous grief and his tiny poems.

In this poem the image of songs that turn into little birds is highly artificial. This makes the poem, lovely as it is, subject to parody, a fact that Heine recognized. Before it was even published, he himself wrote a lampoon, beginning

"Ich mache die kleinen Lieder." He described the snoring husband lying beside his former beloved and the baby boys that they produced together. Heine concluded that he would rather have made little babies than little songs.

"Aus meinen großen Schmerzen" is the 36th poem in *Lyrical Intermezzo.* For more information about that collection of poems, please read the commentary on Mendelssohn's *"Auf Flügeln des Gesanges,"* page 75.

Musical Background

In 1843 Franz sent a set of 12 songs to Robert Schumann, hoping to receive his comments and approval. Schumann liked them so much that he gave them to a publisher, who printed them without even informing Franz ahead of time. In addition, Schumann published a review of the songs, Franz's Opus 1, praising them warmly without mentioning his role in their publication. Although Schumann mentioned a few ways in which the songs could have been better, he delivered a memorable judgment about the intensely personal quality of Franz's songs: "The delivery of these songs requires singers, poets, human beings; it would be best to sing them alone and then surely in the evening hours."

Schumann advised Franz not to become a miniaturist, but that is exactly what he became. He published 279 songs and practically nothing else. Furthermore, limiting his own subject matter, he said, "My songs are not meant to arouse, but to create peace and tranquility."

Franz often began songs without any piano introduction and gave them short postludes or none at all. He always used the voice in a lyrical, never in a declamatory way. He wrote meticulously for the piano, voicing each chord with great care. This song could be quite enjoyably played as a piano solo.

Notice that there is a *ritardando* at the end of the first stanza but not the second because the tempo must continue into the piano postlude.

Sources

Text first published in: *Tragödien, nebst einem lyrischen Intermezzo.* Berlin, 1823. *Lyrisches Intermezzo* was also published in *Buch der Lieder*, 1827. This version: *Heine Säkularausgabe, Gedichte, 1812–1827*, vol. 1. Berlin: Akademie-Verlag, 1979.

Music: *12 Gesänge*, Opus 5, no. 1. Leipzig: Whistling, 1846. Original key: F Major.

Aus meinen großen Schmerzen

H. Heine

Robert Franz

(Range: C#4 – E5)

Aus mei-nen gro-ßen Schmer-zen mach' ich die klei-nen

Lie - der; die he - ben ihr klin - gend Ge - fie - der und

flat - tern nach ih - rem Her - zen. Sie

ⓐ "Sincerely." Suggestion: ♪ = 76

Translation: Out of my great sorrows I make little songs. They lift their wings and flutter to where she is.

fan - den den Weg zur Trau - ten, doch kom - men sie wie - der und kla - gen, und

kla - gen, und wol - len nicht sa - gen, was sie___ im Her - zen

schau - ten.

They found the way to my beloved, but they came back, wailing. They wail and don't want to tell me what they saw in her heart.

Im Herbst

[ɪm hɛrpst]

In the Autumn

Robert Franz (1815–1892)

di: h̲aedə ɪst braon aenst bly:tə   zi: ro:t
1. **Die Heide ist braun, einst blühte   sie rot;**
   The heath is   brown; once bloomed it red;

di: bɪrkə ɪst ka:l gry:n va:r aenst i:r klaet
2. **Die Birke ist kahl, grün war einst ihr Kleid;**
   the birch is bare; green was once its dress;

aenst gɪŋ   ɪç ʦu: ʦvaen jɛʦt ge: ɪç all̲aen
3. **Einst ging   ich zu zwei'n, jetzt geh' ich allein,**
   once walked I in a-pair, now walk I   alone,

ve: y:bər den hɛrpst ʊnt di: gra:mfɔllə ʦaet o: ve:
4. **Weh' über den Herbst und die gramvolle Zeit! O weh!**
   alas for   the autumn and the sorrowful   time! Oh, alas!

aenst bly:tən di: ro:zən jɛʦt vɛlkən zi: all
5. **Einst blühten die Rosen, jetzt welken sie all',**
   Once bloomed the roses, now wither they all;

fɔll   dʊft   wa:r di: blu:mə nu:n ʦo:k e:r hɛra̲os
6. **Voll Duft   war die Blume, nun zog   er heraus;**
   full-of fragrance was the flower, now went it away.

aenst pflʏkt ɪç ʦu: ʦvaen jɛʦt pflʏk ɪç all̲aen
7. **Einst pflückt' ich zu zwei'n, jetzt pflück' ich allein;**
   Once picked I in a-pair, now pick I   alone;

das vɪrt   aen dʏrrər   aen du̲ftlo:zər straos
8. **Das wird   ein dürrer, ein duftloser Strauß!**
   That will-be a   withered, a   scentless bouquet!

di vɛlt ɪst zo: ʔø:t   zi: wa:r aenst zo: ʃø:n
9. **Die Welt ist so öd',   sie war einst so schön;**
   The world is so barren, it was once so beautiful;

ɪç va:r aenst zo: raeç jɛʦt bɪn ɪç fɔll   no:t
10. **Ich war einst so reich, jetzt bin ich voll   Not!**
    I   was once so rich, now am I full-of need!

11. **Einst ging ich zu zwei'n, jetzt geh' ich allein!**

maen li:p   ɪst falʃ   o: vɛ:rə ɪç to:t
12. **Mein' Lieb' ist falsch, o wäre ich tot!**
    My   love is false, oh, were I   dead!

Wolfgang Müller (1816–1873)
[vɔlfgaŋ mʏllər]

Poetic Background

"In springtime we were happy here, but my lover has betrayed me. I wish I were dead."

The poet has been forgotten except that Schumann set one of his poems to music and Franz set three. Aside from *"Im Herbst,"* Müller wrote the poems of Franz's *"Im Walde"* and his most famous song of all, *"Widmung (O danke nicht für diese Lieder)."* (Note that Wolfgang Müller is not Wilhelm Müller, the poet of Schubert's *Die schöne Müllerin* and *Die Winterreise.*)

Line 1: *Heide* is a wild landscape covered with low shrubs, a heath. *Heide* is also a name used for various wild shrubs, heather.

Line 3: *zu zweien* means "there were two of us." It would be more logical to say "We walked in a pair,. . ." but the poet emphasizes his loneliness by saying, "I . . ."

Line 6: *zog* is the past tense of *ziehen*, which can express almost any form of movement. The subject pronoun *er* stands for *der Duft*.

Line 8: *wird* stands for *wird. . . sein*, will be.

Musical Background

Hopeless gloom surrounds this song, but the mood is not merely depression. The powerful melody, with its wide range and surging, scalewise phrases, reveals the poet's anger over the destruction of his past happiness.

Hermann Reutter, himself a great song composer and accompanist, wrote about the climax of this song: ". . . the last verse contains what I can only describe as a flash of genius; at the words *"Mein' Lieb' ist falsch"* the dreadful word *"falsch"* is accompanied not by a dissonance but by an inversion of the Neapolitan sixth chord, a consonance which is more mordant and penetrating than even the most grinding discord." (in *Voice*, edited by Sir Keith Falkner. London: Macdonald, 1983.)

Sources

Text: Franz may have taken the text from *Junge Lieder*, 1841, or from *Gedichte*, 1847.

Music: *6 Gesänge*, Opus 17, No. 6. Leipzig: C. F. W. Siegel, between 1852–59. Original key: C minor.

Im Herbst

Wolfgang Müller

Robert Franz
(Range: C4 – A♭5)

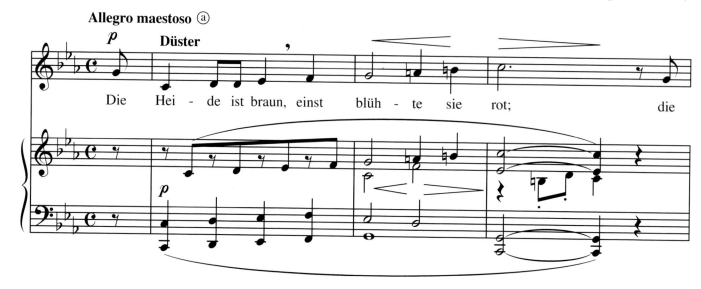

Allegro maestoso ⓐ

Düster

Die Hei - de ist braun, einst blüh - te sie rot; die

Bir - ke ist kahl, grün war einst ihr Kleid; einst

ging ich zu zwei'n, jetzt geh'___ ich al - lein;

ⓐ Suggestion: ♩ = ca. 96 (with frequent use of rubato). *"Düster"* (dark, gloomy) is a mood or style marking.
ⓑ Pianist's right hand crosses under the left hand.

Translation: The heath is brown; once it bloomed red. The birch is bare; once it was dressed in green. Once we walked as a pair; now I walk alone.

Alas for the autumn and the sorrowful time! Once the roses were blooming; now they are all withered. Their blooms were full of fragrance; now it is all gone. Once

we gathered flowers as a pair; now I do so alone. That will be a withered, scentless bouquet. The world is so barren, once it was so beautiful. I

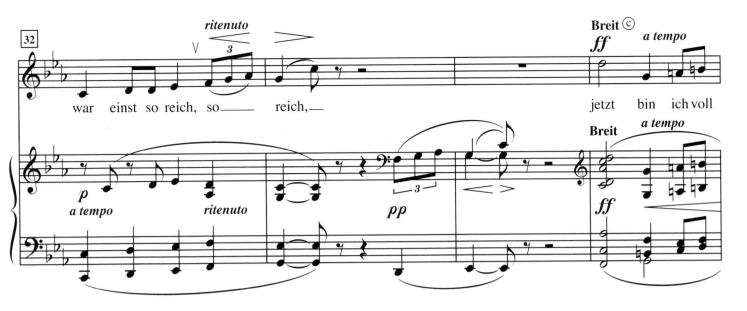

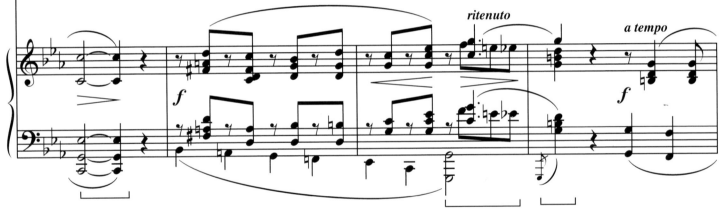

ⓒ "Breit," broadly.

ⓓ "Sehr leiderschaftlich," very passionately.

ⓔ Some editions indicate *allargando* for the last two phrases, but this is not from Franz.

was once so rich, now I am in need! Once we walked as a pair; now I walk alone. My love is false; if only I were dead!

Liebst du um Schönheit

If You Love for Beauty's Sake

Clara Schumann (1819–1896)
[klɑ:ra ʃu:man]

li:pst du: ʊm ʃøːnhaet
1. Liebst du um Schönheit,
If-love you for beauty,

oː nɪçt mɪç li̠:bə
2. O nicht mich liebe!
oh, not me love!

li̠:bə di: zɔnnə
3. Liebe die Sonne,
Love the sun,

zi: trɛːkt aen gɔltnəs hɑːr
4. Sie trägt ein goldnes Haar!
it wears [a] golden hair!

li:pst du ʊm ju̠:gənt
5. Liebst du um Jugend,
If-love you for youth,

6. O nicht mich liebe!

li̠:bə den fry̠:lɪŋ
7. Liebe den Frühling,
Love the spring,

der   ju̠ŋ   ɪst je̠ːdəs jɑːr
8. Der   jung ist jedes Jahr!
which young is every year!

li:pst du: ʊm ʃɛ̠tsə
9. Liebst du um Schätze,
If-love you for treasures,

10. O nicht mich liebe!

li̠:bə di: me̠ːrfrao
11. Liebe die Meerfrau,
love the mermaid,

zi: hat fiːl pɛ̠rlən klɑːr
12. Sie hat viel Perlen klar!
she has many pearls bright!

li:pst du: ʊm li̠:bə
13. Liebst du um Liebe,
If-love you for love,

oː jɑː mɪç li̠:bə
14. O ja— mich liebe!
oh, yes, me   love!

li̠:bə mɪç ɪmmər
15. Liebe mich immer,
Love me always,

dɪç li:b ɪç ɪmmərdɑːr
16. Dich lieb' ich immerdar!
you love I   forever!

Friedrich Rückert (1788–1866)

Poetic Background

"I have nothing to offer but love— a boundless supply!"

Rückert's devotion to Middle Eastern poetry was mentioned (page 49) in the commentary to Schubert's *"Lachen und Weinen."* His love for his bride Luise was mentioned (page 85) in the commentary before Schumann's *"Widmung."* In Rückert's large collection of poems entitled *Liebesfrühling* (Springtime of Love), this poem is in the section called *Wiedergewonnen* (Won Again). The poem has four stanzas of four lines each.

Line 4: *Haar* can mean one hair or a whole head of hair, as in English.

Musical Background

Following a long legal battle with Clara's father, Robert and Clara succeeded in marrying in 1840. All through the challenges, complications and eventual bliss of that year Robert was composing songs, at least 127 in that year alone. Clara also composed three songs as her Christmas gift to her new husband.

In 1841 Robert composed six songs and three duets from *Liebesfrühling* and then persuaded Clara to write three more songs so that all twelve pieces could be published together as one book. The first edition bore two opus numbers: it was Robert's Opus 37 and Clara's Opus 12. Because Robert enjoyed mystifying critics, the first edition had no indication which songs were his and which were hers.

It is natural to expect that stylistic traits of Robert's songs show up also in Clara's: for instance, the use of *ritardando* with no indication when to resume the main tempo; the piano taking over the melody as in mm 15–16; and the long and expressive piano postlude. But Clara deserves full credit for the gracefulness of the melody and the sensitive way in which the fourth stanza is varied and extended.

Sources

Text: *Ausgewählte Werke. Liebesfrühling.* Frankfurt: Sauerländer, 1872.

Music: *Zwölf Gedichte aus F. Rückert's "Liebesfrühling,"* Opus 12, no. 4. Leipzig: Breitkopf & Härtel, 1841. Original key: D♭.

Liebst du um Schönheit

F. Rückert

Clara Schumann
(Range: F4 – E♭5)

Liebst du um Schön- heit, o nicht mich lie - be!

Lie - be die Son - ne, sie

ⓐ "Not too slow." Suggestion: ♩ = ca. 80

Translation: If you love for beauty's sake, don't love me! Love the sun who

ⓑ *A tempo.*

has golden hair. If you love for the sake of youth, don't love me! Love the spring that is new every year.
If you love

© "More motion."

for treasures' sake, don't love me! Love the mermaid who has many bright pearls. If you love for love's sake, yes, love

lie - be! Liebst du um Lie - be, o ja— mich lie - be,

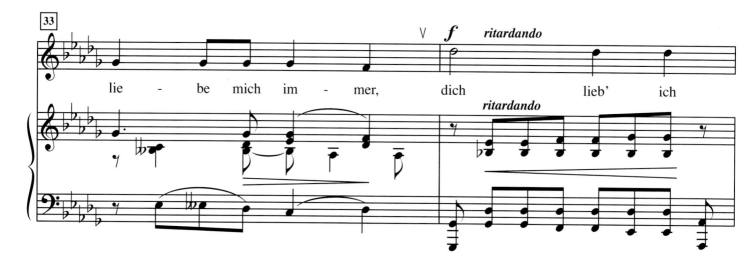

lie - be mich im - mer, dich lieb' ich

im - mer - dar!

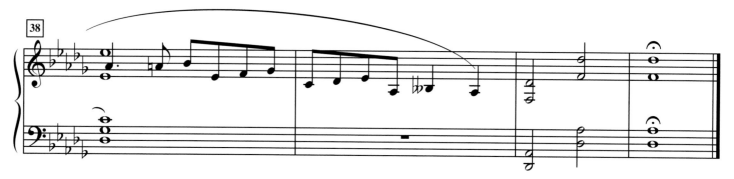

me! Love me forever; I love you forevermore.

Ein Ton
A Tone

Peter Cornelius (1824–1874)

[pe̠ːtər kɔrne̠ːli̯ʊs]

miːr	klɪŋt	aen	toːn	zoː	vʊndərbɑːr

1. Mir   klingt   ein   Ton   so   wunderbar

To-me rings a tone so wonderful

ɪn	hɛrts	ʊnt	zɪnnən	ɪmmərdɑːr

2. In Herz und Sinnen immerdar.

in heart and mind forevermore.

ɪst	ɛs	aen	hɑox	der	diːr	ɛntʃveːpt

3. Ist es ein   Hauch,   der dir   entschwebt,

Is it a breath that from-you wafted-away

als	a̠enmɑːl	nɔx	daen	mʊnt	gəbe̠ːpt

4. Als einmal   noch dein   Mund gebebt?

as once still your mouth trembled?

ɪst	ɛs	dɛs	glœklaens	tryːbər	klaŋ

5. Ist es des Glöckleins trüber   Klang,

Is it the little-bells dismal ring

der	diːr	gəfo̠lkt	den	veːk	ɛntlaŋ

6. Der   dir gefolgt   den Weg entlang?

which you followed the road along?

miːr	klɪŋt	der	toːn	zoː	vɔl	ʊnt	raen

7. Mir   klingt der Ton so   voll und rein,

To-me rings the tone so full, so pure,

als	ʃlœs	er	da̠enə	ze̠ːlə	ʔaen

8. Als   schlöss' er deine   Seele ein,

as-if enclosed it your soul within,

als	ʃti̠ːgəst	li̠ːbənt	ni̠ːdər	duː

9 Als   stiegest liebend nieder   du

as-if climbed lovingly downward you

ʊnt	zɛ̠ŋəst	ma̠enən	ʃmɛrts	ɪn	ruː

10. Und sängest meinen   Schmerz in Ruh'.

and sang my pain to rest.

Poetic Background

"In imagination I hear a lovely tone repeating like a message of comfort from you, my departed love."

Like the Elizabethan writers of lute songs, Cornelius wrote both the poetry and the music of most of his songs, including this one. Only a few composers in the past centuries have made a habit of writing their own texts.

In a letter to a friend, Hugo Wolf wrote about the poetry of Cornelius: "I cannot read enough of him. He is one of the truest poets that the Germans have— and fail to appreciate." (Quoted by Susan Youens in *Hugo Wolf: The Vocal Music*.)

Lines 3 and 4: *entschwebt* and *gebebt* are both participles; in both cases the auxiliary verb is understood.

Line 5: *Glöckleins*, in the context of a funeral, means a "passing bell," a small bell that is kept tolling continually in a church while a parishioner is dying, as a call to prayer.

Line 9: *nieder*, downward, from Heaven, where the departed one dwells.

Musical Background

In the autumn of 1854 Cornelius wrote both text and music of a cycle of six songs, *Trauer und Trost* (Mourning and Comfort).

In this song Cornelius represents a mental obsession, a grief that penetrates every moment of the singer's life. The singer sustains one pitch throughout the song, while the accompaniment changes harmonies and even changes keys. Technically, this tone is called a pedal tone, named from the frequent use of this device in organ music, where a pedal can be held down while the hands are playing changing harmonies.

The emotional climax is identified by the point at which the pedal tone is the most dissonant with the chord in the accompaniment, mm24–26. The chord is written with an augmented sixth, but if the two upper tones of the chord are re-spelled enharmonically, the pedal tone is the ninth of a ninth chord in root position. The ninth chord remains unresolved and the two upper tones are used in m27 as the common tones for a modulation to the tonic major key.

The shifting harmonies of this song create such a satisfying piece of music that listeners sometimes fail to notice the lack of conventional melody. In the absence of any melodic movement, the text must be sung with subtle timing and inflection.

Sources

Text: *Literarische Werke*, Volume IV: *Gedichte*. Leipzig: Breitkopf und Härtel, 1905. (Reprint: New York: Johnson Reprint, 1960.)

Music: *Trauer und Trost, Opus 3, no. 3*. The autograph is in the possession of an anonymous collector. First edition: Mainz: Schott, between 1852–59. Original key: E minor.

Ein Ton

P. Cornelius

Peter Cornelius
(Range: B4)

ⓐ "Somewhat animated." Suggestion: ♩= ca. 69

Translation: A wonderful tone rings in my heart and imagination constantly. Is it a breath that issued from your mouth when you were still

bebt?_____   Ist es des Glöck-leins trü - ber

Klang,   der dir ge-folgt den Weg   ent-lang?

Mir   klingt der Ton   so voll und   rein,   als schlöss' er

dei - ne See - le ein,_____

living? Is it the dismal passing bell that followed your coffin along the road? The tone seems as full, as pure to me as if it contained your whole soul,

als stie-gest lie - bend nie-der Du und sän-gest mei-nen Schmerz in

Ruh'.

as if you were climbing down to me lovingly and singing my pain to rest.

Die Mainacht

[diː ˈmaenaxt]

May Night

Johannes Brahms (1833–1897)

[johanəs braːms]

van	der	zɪlbərnə moːnt	dʊrç	diː	gəʃtrɔøçə	blɪŋkt
1. Wann	**der**	**silberne Mond**	**durch**	**die**	**Gesträuche**	**blinkt**
When	the	silvery moon	through	the	shrubbery	flashes

ʊnt	zaen	ʃlʊmmərndəs	lɪçt	yːbər den raːzən	ʃtrɔøt
2. Und	**sein**	**schlummerndes**	**Licht**	**über den Rasen**	**streut,**
and	its	slumbering	light	over the lawn	spreads,

ʊnt	diː naxtɪgal	fløːtət
3. Und	**die Nachtigall**	**flötet,**
and	the nightingale	sings,

vandl	ɪç	traorɪç	fɔn bʊʃ	tsuː	bʊʃ
4. Wandl'	**ich**	**traurig**	**von Busch**	**zu**	**Busch.**
wander	I	sadly	from bush	to	bush.

yːbərhYllət	fɔm laop	gɪrrət	aen	taobənpaːr
5. Überhüllet	**vom Laub**	**girret**	**ein**	**Taubenpaar**
Covered-over	by leaves	coos	a	dove-pair

zaen	ɛnttsYkən	miːr foːr	aːbər	ɪç vɛndə	mɪç
6. sein	**Entzücken**	**mir vor;**	**aber**	**ich wende**	**mich,**
its	delight	to-me aloud,	but	I turn	myself,

zuːxə	dʊŋklərə	ʃatən
7. suche	**dunklere**	**Schatten,**
seek	darker	shadows,

ʊnt diː	ʔaenzaːmə	trɛːnə	rɪnt
8. und die	**einsame**	**Träne**	**rinnt.**
and the	lonely	tear	runs.

van	o lɛçəlndəs	bɪlt	vɛlçəs	viː	mɔrgənroːt
9. Wann,	**o lächelndes**	**Bild,**	**welches**	**wie**	**Morgenrot**
When,	o smiling	image,	which	like	morning-red

dʊrç	diː zeːlə	miːr	ʃtraːlt,	fɪnt	ɪç aof eːrdən	dɪç
10. Durch	**die Seele**	**mir**	**strahlt,**	**find'**	**ich auf Erden**	**dich?**
through	the soul	to-me	radiates,	find	I on earth	you?

11. Und die einsame Träne

beːpt	miːr	haesər	diː vaŋ	hɛrap
12. Bebt	**mir**	**heißer**	**die Wang'**	**herab.**
trembles	to-me	more-hotly	the cheek	downward.

Ludwig Heinrich Christoph Hölty (1748–1776)

Poetic Background

"Grieving for my lost love, I walk in a garden at night. The cooing of happy doves reminds me how great is my loss and brings me to tears."

In *"Seligkeit"* (page 37) Hölty expressed the hopefulness of love, but his hopes were not fulfilled. This poem, written a year later, expresses despair. Unfortunately, Hölty died of tuberculosis at age 28, not having experienced a happy love.

Like other poets of his time, Hölty liked to use ancient Greek metric forms. Greek verse is not based on rhyme or on stress patterns, but on patterns of long and short vowels. When these forms are used in German, stressed syllables replace the long vowels and unstressed syllables replace the short ones. Each of the four stanzas of *"Die Mainacht"* is in a form called an Asclepiadic ode, which can be charted this way:

(/ = stressed, _ = unstressed, ' = caesura)

```
/ _ / _ _ / ' / _ _ / _ /
/ _ / _ _ / ' / _ _ / _ /
/ _ / _ _ / _
/ _ / _ _ / _ /
```

Brahms used a version of the poem edited by Hölty's friend, J. H. Voss, in 1804 for publication. Voss made word changes in the poem, but the song is so famous that it is not advisable to restore Hölty's original words. Brahms omitted the second stanza.

Line 1: *Wann*, Hölty wrote *wenn* (same meaning); *blinkt*, Hölty wrote *blickt* (looks).

Line 2: *schlummerndes Licht*, an imaginative word choice for light that shines when most of the world is asleep; *streut*, Hölty wrote *geußt* (pours), a word that is now obsolete.

Line 3: *dunklere Schatten*, Hölty wrote *dunkle Gesträuche* (dark shrubbery).

Line 4: *wandl'* comes from *wandeln*, which means to walk slowly, without a particular goal.

Musical Background

Hölty, born near Hanover, and Brahms, born in Hamburg, were both North Germans, with a stereotypical undercurrent of melancholy and introspection.

Brahms wrote *"Die Mainacht"* in Karlsruhe in April, 1866. He habitually kept his songs in manuscript for awhile to revise them. He did not consider them finished until they had been engraved and he made final revisions on the proofs.

"Die Mainacht" deserves its fame as an example of everything that is finest in Brahms's songs: harmonic richness, sweeping melody, formal clarity. Analysis cannot explain romantic magic, but we can admire Brahms's craft. He portrays the poet's wandering in darkness by avoiding root position harmonies, the doves' gentle cooing by moving the piano part to the treble range, the surge of sudden grief by triplet arpeggios in the bass.

The listener clearly hears the first stanza (A) and a contrasting second stanza (B) before the third stanza takes up the first melody again, intensified by triplets in the accompaniment (A').

But after only six measures, the second occurrence of the words *"Und die einsame Träne. . ."* brings back music from the B section, (measures 39–42). This time the melody is extended over subdominant and Neapolitan harmonies to its despairing end. The postlude returns to the calm of nature, untouched by the poet's grief.

The first performance was sung by Julius Stockhausen with Brahms in Hamburg, March 11, 1868.

Schubert used all four stanzas of *"Die Mainacht"* for a charming strophic song (D. 194). Fanny Hensel used only two stanzas in her poignant setting (Opus 9, no. 6).

Sources

Text: Hölty's manuscript (May, 1774) is reproduced in: *Ludwig Heinrich Christoph Hölty: Leben und Werk.* Hannover: Schlüter, 1986. First publication: *Göttinger Musenalmanach 1775*, page 210.

Music: *Vier Gesänge,* Opus 43, No.2. Leipzig: Rieter-Biedermann, 1868. Original key: E♭.

Die Mainacht

L. H. C. Hölty

Johannes Brahms
(Range: C4 – G♭5)

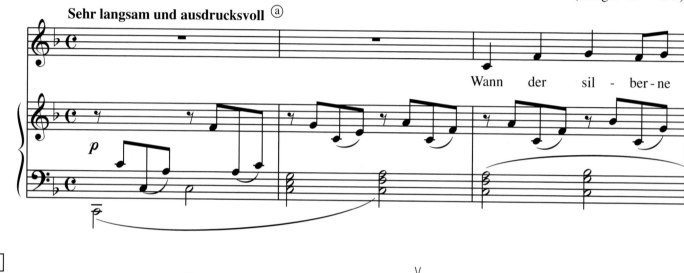

ⓐ "Very slowly and expressively." Suggestion: ♩ = ca. 60

Translation: When the silver moon shines through the trees and spreads its slumbrous light over the grass and the nightingale

flö - tet, wandl' ich trau - rig von Busch zu

Busch. Ü - ber - hül - let vom

Laub gir - ret ein Tau - ben - paar sein Ent - zü - cken mir

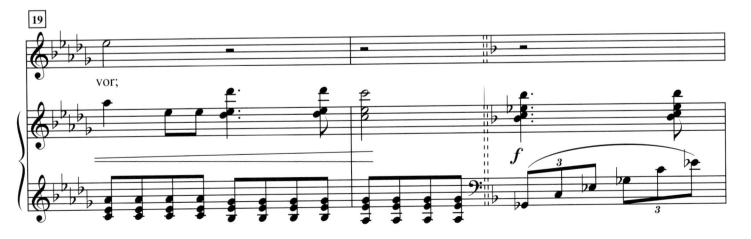

vor;

sings, I wander sadly from bush to bush. Concealed by the leaves, a pair of doves coos its delight for me to hear;

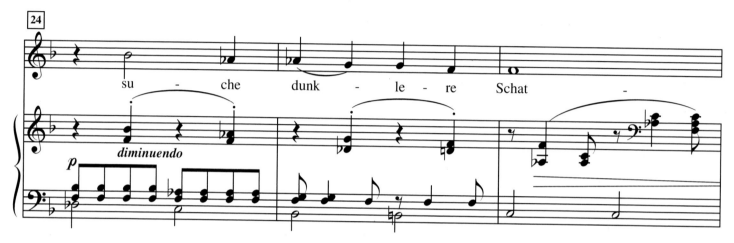

but I turn away and seek darker shadows. And the lonely tear runs.

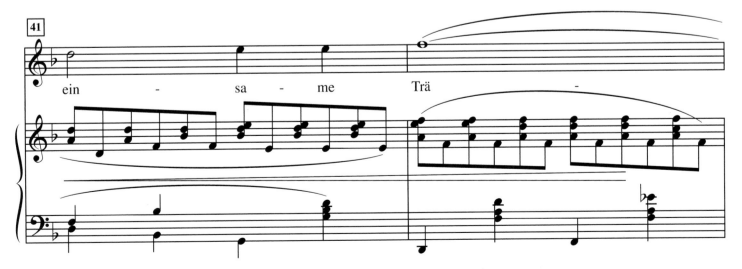

O smiling image that like a rosy dawn radiates through my soul, when will I find you on earth? And the lonely tear

trembles, hot, running down my cheek.

Wiegenlied

[viːgənliːt]

Lullaby

Johannes Brahms (1833–1897)

guːtən ʔɑːbənt guːt naxt
1. Guten Abend, gut' Nacht,
Good   evening, good night,

mɪt roːzən bədaxt
2. Mit Rosen bedacht,
with roses   roofed-over

mɪt nɛːglaen bəʃtɛkt
3. Mit Näg'lein besteckt,
with lilacs   embroidered,

ʃlʊpf   ʊntər diː dɛk
4. Schlupf' unter die Deck':
slip   under the cover:

mɔrgən fryː vɛn gɔt vɪl
5. Morgen früh, wenn Gott will,
morning early, if   God wills,

vɪrst duː viːdər gəvɛkt
6. Wirst du wieder geweckt.
will   you again   be-awakened.

7. Guten Abend, gut Nacht,

fɔn ɛŋlaen bəvaxt
8. Von Englein bewacht,
by angels   guarded,

diː tsaegən ɪm traom
9. Die zeigen   im Traum
who will-show in   dream

diːr krɪstkɪntlaens baom
10. Dir   Christkindlein's Baum.
to-you Christ-child's   tree.

ʃlɑːf   nuːn zeːlɪç   ʊnt zyːs
11. Schlaf' nun selig   und süß,
Sleep   now blissfully and sweetly,

ʃao ɪm traoms paradiːs
12. Schau im   Traum's Paradies.
see   in-the dream-the Paradise.

First stanza, from *Des Knaben Wunderhorn*
Second stanza by Georg Scherer (1828–1909)

Poetic Background

"Sleep sweetly, my baby, and dream of a Christmas tree and of Paradise."

Many versions of this poem exist, some of them going back to the 15th century. Arnim and Brentano printed this version in *Des Knaben Wunderhorn* with the title *"Gute Nacht, mein Kind!"* (Good Night, My Child). It consists of only one six-line stanza. In order to lengthen the song, Brahms's publisher proposed using Georg Scherer's pre-existing verse.

Line 1: *gut*, in the published poem *gute*.

Line 2: *bedacht* is an old variant of *bedeckt* (covered). Lines 2 and 3 refer to flowers embroidered on the baby's bedspread.

Line 3: *Näglein* are lilac blossoms, according to one authority, or carnations (*Nelken*), according to another.

Line 4: *schlupf'* is an unusual form of *schlüpfen*. *Deck'* is shortened from *Decke* (bedspread).

Line 5: *wenn*, in the published poem *wenn's Gott will*, if God wills it.

Line 10: *Christkindlein's Baum* is a Christmas tree. Gifts found under it are gifts from the Christ Child, not from St. Nicholas.

Line 12: *'s* is contracted from *das*, because *Paradies* is a neuter noun. This slight awkwardness occurred because Scherer's poem did not exactly fit the rhythm of the melody.

Musical Background

As the conductor of a women's chorus in Hamburg in 1859 Brahms had flirtations with several of the young singers. One was Bertha Porubsky, who liked to sing a certain Viennese waltz song. She became Frau Bertha Faber and moved to Vienna. When she gave birth to her second son in July, 1868, Brahms was in Bonn. He wrote a lullaby for her to sing to the baby and quoted the tune of her favorite waltz in the piano introduction. He dedicated the song to her, "B. F."

1868 was also the year when Brahms permanently settled in Vienna, following years when he had moved frequently, either to find employment or to be with one or another of his friends. He still toured as a pianist, but usually only for performances of his own works.

We can hardly imagine the world without "the Brahms lullaby," and yet the melody is quite unusual for a cradle song. Most slumber songs feature stepwise downward movement but this one has many upward leaps and even an upward cadence.

The first public performance was given by Louise Dustmann and Clara Schumann in Vienna on December 22, 1869.

Sources

Text: Arnim & Brentano, *Des Knaben Wunderhorn, alte deutsche Lieder*. Volume 3. Heidelberg: Mohr & Winter, second edition, 1819.

Music: *Fünf Lieder*, Opus 49, no. 4. Berlin: Simrock, October 1868. Original key: E♭ (but Brahms wanted it published in F).

Wiegenlied

Des Knaben Wunderhorn; **G. Scherer**

Johannes Brahms
(Range: E♭4 – E♭5)

Gu-ten A - bend, gut' Nacht, mit_ Ro - sen be-

dacht,_ mit_ Näg' - lein be - steckt, schlupf'_ un - ter die Deck': mor - gen

früh, wenn Gott will, wirst du wie - der ge - weckt, mor - gen früh, wenn Gott

ⓐ "Gently moving." Suggestion: ♩ = ca. 82
ⓑ The grace note is usually sung quickly, on the beat.

Translation: Good evening, good night! Slip under the covers embroidered with roses and lilacs. Tomorrow morning,
God willing,

will,   wirst du   wie - der ge - weckt.   Gu - ten

A - bend, gut' Nacht,   von _ Eng - lein be - wacht, _ die _ zei - gen im _

Traum   dir _   Christ - kind - lein's Baum. Schlaf' nun se - lig und süß,   schau im

Traum's Pa - ra - dies, schlaf' nun se - lig und süß,   schau im Traum's Pa - ra - dies.

© The double grace notes take part of the time of the preceding quarter. They should be sung as quickly and as late as possible, provided they are clear.

you will wake up again. Good evening, good night, watched by angels, dreaming of a Christmas tree. Sleep now blissfully and sweetly, and see Heaven in your dream.

O kühler Wald

Oh Cool Forest

Johannes Brahms (1833–1897)

oː kyːlər valt
1. O kühler Wald,
Oh cool   forest,

voː rɑoʃəst‿ duː
2. Wo rauschest du,
where rustle   you

ɪn dem maen liːpçən geːt
3. In dem mein Liebchen geht?
in which my   darling   walks?

oː viːdərhall
4. O Widerhall,
Oh echo,

voː lɑoʃəst‿ duː
5. Wo lauschest du,
where listen   you

der gɛrn maen liːt fɛrʃteːt
6. Der gern mein Lied versteht?
which gladly my   song understands?

ɪm hɛrtsən tiːf
7. Im Herzen tief,
In-the heart   deep,

dɑː rɑoʃt‿ der valt
8. Da rauscht der Wald,
there rustles   the forest

9. In dem mein Liebchen geht;

ɪn ʃmɛrtsən ʃliːf
10. In Schmerzen schlief
in pains   slept

der viːdərhal
11. Der Widerhall,
the echo,

diː liːdər zint fɛrveːt
12. Die Lieder sind verweht.
the songs   are   drifted-away.

Clemens Brentano (1778–1842)
[kleːməns brɛntɑːno]

Poetic Background

"The forest where we lovers walked, the lovesongs that I sang, are all gone. They exist now only in my heart."

Brentano's poem crystallizes several themes of Romanticism: a forest; an absent lover; an echo that does not just repeat the poet's songs but even "understands" them.

The poem has four six-line stanzas; Brahms used only the first and third.

Musical Background

When Brahms composed *"O kühler Wald"* in March 1877, he was a mature master, one of Europe's most prominent composers. His first symphony had had a triumphant premiere six months before. Living mainly on royalties from his publisher, he kept a comfortable Viennese bachelor apartment and spent summers in Italy.

Brahms wrote many strophic songs but more characteristic of him are the many songs like this one, in which each stanza is varied in a unique way. In *"O kühler Wald"* all motion seems to stop at the end of the first stanza. The second begins with two measures of magical stillness before the true return of the first melody, its forward motion enhanced by the varied accompaniment. Only with the repetition of the final line does the motion slow again, not with a ritardando but by adding an extra beat to each of the last three measures.

The first public performance was given by Adele Assmann in Breslau on October 22, 1878.

Sources

Text: *Gesammelte Werke* (Frankfurt, 1852–55).
Music: *Fünf Gesänge*, Opus 72, No. 3. Berlin: Simrock, 1877. Original key: A♭.

O kühler Wald

C. Brentano

Johannes Brahms
(Range: E4 – F5 or G5)

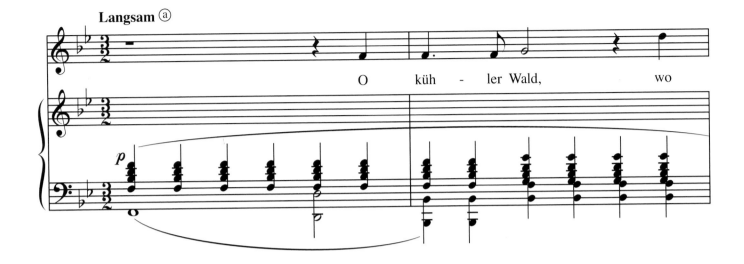

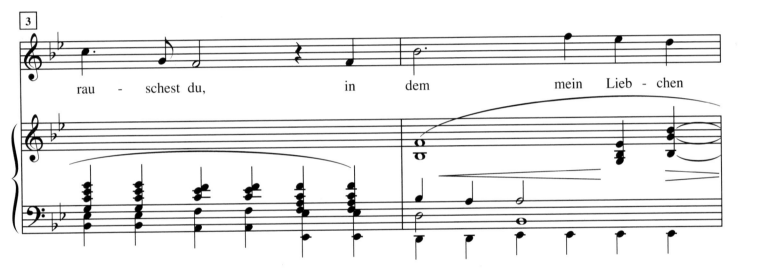

ⓐ "Slowly." Suggestion: ♩ = ca. 48

Translation: O cool forest in which my beloved is walking, where

ⓑ Brahms provided the optional high note. One may infer that he preferred the high note but did not want to insist on having it.

are you softly whispering? O echo that happily understands my song, where are you poised to listen? Deep in my heart— there is the whispering forest where my beloved

is walking. Surrounded by pain, the echo fell asleep, the songs have drifted away.

Vergebliches Ständchen

[fɛrgeːplɪçəs ʃtɛntçən]
Vain Serenade

Johannes Brahms (1833–1897)

guːtən ʔɑːbənt maen ʃats
1. Guten Abend, mein Schatz,
Good   evening, my   treasure,

guːtən ʔɑːbənt maen kɪnt
2. Guten Abend, mein Kind!
good   evening, my   child!

ɪç kɔm ɑos liːp tsu diːr
3. Ich komm' aus Lieb' zu dir,
I   come   from love to   you;

ax max miːr ʔɑof diː tyːr
4. Ach, mach' mir   auf die Tür!
ah   make for-me open the door!

5. Mach' mir auf die Tür!

maen tyːr ɪst fɛrʃlɔsən
6. "Mein' Tür ist verschlossen,
"My   door is   locked;

ɪç las dɪç nɪçt ʔaen
7. Ich lass dich nicht ein;
I   let   you   not   in.

muttər diː rɛːt   miːr kluːk
8. Mut-ter die rät   mir klug,
Mother she advises me   cleverly,

vɛːrst duː hɛraen mɪt fuːk
9. Wär'st du herein mit Fug,
were   you in-here with right,

vɛːrs mɪt miːr foːrbae
10. Wär's mit mir vorbei!"
were-it with me   gone!"

zoː kalt ɪst diː naxt
11. So kalt ist die Nacht,
So cold is   the night,

zoː ʔaezɪç der vɪnt
12. So eisig   der Wind,
so   icy   the wind,

das miːr   das hɛrts ɛrfriːrt
13. Dass mir   das Herz erfriert,
that for-me the heart freezes,

maen liːp ɛrlœʃən vɪrt
14. Mein' Lieb' erlöschen wird;
my   love burn-out will.

œfnə miːr   maen kɪnt
15. Öffne mir,   mein Kind!
Open to-me, my   child!

lœʃət   daen liːp
16. "Löschet   dein Lieb',
"If-burns-out your love,

las ziː lœʃən nuːr
17. Lass sie löschen nur!
let   it   burn-out only!

lœʃət   ziː ɪmmər tsu
18. Löschet   sie immer zu,
If-burns-out it   always more,

geː haem tsu bɛt tsuːr ruː
19. Geh' heim zu Bett zur Ruh',
go   home to bed, to   rest.

guːtə naxt   maen knɑːp
20. Gute Nacht, mein Knab'!"
Good night, my   boy!"

Anton von Zuccalmaglio (1803–18
[ʔantoːn fɔn tsʊkalmaljo]

Poetic Background

He says: "Let me in; we'll have fun!" She says: "Nothing doing; go home!"

Zuccalmaglio wrote down folk songs wherever he heard them, but he liked to rewrite them entirely before publishing them. *"Vergebliches Ständchen"* was published as "folksong from the Lower Rhine region," but only lines 3 and 4 come from a genuine folk song; the rest of the poem is pure Zuccalmaglio. Brahms, in his real enthusiasm for German folk songs, accepted many of Zuccalmaglio's works as if they were a national treasure. In this case he accepted the words but ignored the simple melody that went with them.

Line 4: *auf* is part of the verb *aufmachen* (open). Correct word order would place *auf* at the end of the clause.

Line 5, while repetitious, portrays the young man's urgency. All of the repetitions in this song are also in the original poem, as shown by the fact that each of the four stanzas has five lines.

Line 6: *Mein'*, in the poem *Meine*.

Line 8: *Mutter die* is a folksy construction.

Line 9: *mit Fug*, with legal right, meaning that the boy came in with the girl's permission. (This learned expression sounds inappropriate in a "folk song.")

Line 18: *Löschet*, because it is the first word in the sentence, implies the conditional "if." *Immer zu* is an idiom for "more and more."

Line 20: *Knab'* or *Knabe* (boy) is not the way the young lover would describe himself.

Musical Background

True duets provide for two voices to sing together. The five songs in Opus 84 are not duets but dialogue songs, in which two characters participate without singing simultaneously. (An optional second voice part is provided only at the end of the fifth song.) *"Vergebliches Ständchen"* is thoroughly entertaining when sung by one singer, almost as though she were telling the story to her friends on the morning after the late night visit.

Max Friedlaender's book, *Brahms's Lieder*, gives more background information about this song than can be printed here. Brahms considered it one of his best. He wanted a dramatic interpretation, showing the haughtiness of the girl. Brahms added the words *"Er"* and *"Sie"* before the appropriate stanzas. After the words *"Öffne mir, mein Kind"* the piano interlude, marked *lebhafter* (faster), portrays the girl laughing at the boy before she dismisses him.

This song was probably composed on a vacation in Pörtschach, where Brahms summered 1877–1879. The first performance was sung by tenor Gustav Walter in Vienna on February 23, 1883.

Sources

Text: *Deutsche Volkslieder mit ihrer Original-Weisen.* Berlin, 1840.

Music: *Romanzen und Lieder für eine oder zwei Singstimmen*, Opus 84, No. 4. Berlin: Simrock, 1882. Original key: A.

Vergebliches Ständchen

A. von Zuccalmaglio

Johannes Brahms
(Range: E4 – F♯5)

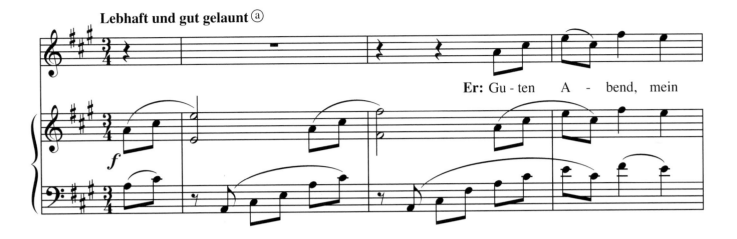

ⓐ "Lively and in a good mood." Suggestion: ♩ = ca.160

Translation: (He says:) Good evening, my dear, good evening, my child. I'm here

Lieb' zu__ dir, ach, mach' mir auf die__ Tür, mach' mir auf die Tür,

mach' mir auf, mach' mir auf, mach' mir auf__ die Tür!

Sie: Mein Tür__ ist ver - schlos-sen, ich lass__ dich nicht ein,

ich lass__ dich nicht ein; Mut - ter die

because I love you! Open the door for me! (She says:) My door is locked, I'm not letting you in. Mother

rät mir klug, wärst du her - ein mit Fug, wär's mit mir vor - bei,

wär's mit mir,   wär's mit mir,   wär's mit mir vor - bei!

Er: So kalt ist die Nacht, so

ei - sig der Wind,   so

gave me good advice: if I allowed you to get in here, it would be all over with me! (He:) The night is so cold, the wind is so icy!

ⓑ "Faster." Most performers infer an *a tempo* at m63.

My heart is freezing, my love is going to cool down! Open up, my child! (She:) If your love is cooling down, just let it!

lö - schen nur,   lass sie lö - schen

nur!   Lö - schet sie im - mer_ zu, geh' heim zu Bett, zur_ Ruh',

gu - te Nacht, mein Knab',   gu - te Nacht,   gu - te Nacht,   gu - te Nacht, mein

Knab'!

Let it cool down some more, and go home to bed. Good night, little boy!

Sapphische Ode

[zapfɪʃə oːdə]
Sapphic Ode

Johannes Brahms (1833–1897)

roːzən	brax	iç	naxts	miːr		am	dʊŋklən	haːgə
1. Rosen	**brach**	**ich**	**nachts**	**mir**		**am**	**dunklen**	**Hage;**
Roses	broke	I	at-night	for-myself		at-the	dark	hedge.

zyːsər	haoxtən	dʊft		ziː	als	jeː	am	taːgə
2. Süßer	**hauchten**	**Duft**		**sie,**	**als**	**je**	**am**	**Tage;**
Sweeter	breathed	fragrance		they	as	ever	by	day;

dɔx	fɛrʃtrɔøtən	raeç	diː	bəveːktən	ɛstə
3. Doch	**verstreuten**	**reich**	**die**	**bewegten**	**Äste**
yet	scattered	richly	the	moved	branches

tao	der	mɪç	nɛstə
4. Tau, der		**mich**	**nässte.**
dew, which		me	moistened.

aox	der	kʏsə	dʊft		mɪç	viː	niː	bərʏktə
5. Auch	**der**	**Küsse**	**Duft**		**mich**	**wie**	**nie**	**berückte,**
Also	the	kisses	fragrance		me	as	never	moved,

diː	iç	naxts	fɔm		ʃtraox	daenər	lɪpən	pflʏktə
6. Die	**ich**	**nachts**	**vom**		**Strauch**	**deiner**	**Lippen**	**pflückte;**
which I		at-night	from-the		branch	of-your	lips	plucked.

dɔx	aox	diːr		bəveːkt	ɪm	gəmyːt	glaeç		jeːnən
7. Doch	**auch**	**dir,**		**bewegt**	**im**	**Gemüt**	**gleich**		**jenen,**
Yet	also	for-you,		moved	in	soul	exactly-like		those,

taotən		diː	trɛːnən
8. Tauten		**die**	**Tränen!**
appeared-like-dew		the	tears.

Hans Schmidt (1854–unknown)
[hans ʃmɪt]

Poetic Background

"When I gathered roses at night, the dew made my sleeve wet. So, too, did your tears when we kissed."

Like the earlier poet, Hölty, Hans Schmidt liked to write in ancient Greek metrical forms. Greek verse is not based on rhyme or on stress patterns, but on patterns of long and short vowels. When these forms are used in German, stressed syllables replace the long vowels and unstressed syllables replace the short ones. The particular metrical form that Schmidt uses here is called a Sapphic ode; each stanza has three lines of eleven syllables followed by a line of five syllables. The stanza is named in honor of the Greek woman poet Sappho, but the content of the poem is not related to her in any way.

Title: *"Gereimte sapphische Ode"* (Rhymed Sapphic Ode) was Schmidt's title. (Rhyme is not usually used in Greek stanza forms.)

Notice that the first P in Sappho's name is spoken in German, but not in English.

Line 7: *jenen* refers to the branches of the rose bush; they were physically moved just as (*gleich*) the beloved was emotionally moved.

Musical Background

According to Friedlaender, the songs of Opus 94 owe their existence to the great baritone Julius Stockhausen, whose concerts Brahms often accompanied at the piano. But the record shows that the first performance of "Sapphische Ode" was sung by tenor Gustav Walter in Vienna on January 9, 1885. It was composed during the preceding summer.

To set the last line of the poem Brahms deliberately quoted from Schubert's song *"Am Meer,"* which also ends with the words *"die Tränen."* The tears in the Schubert song are described as poisonous, but the tears in this song are tears of happy love.

Sources

Text: *Gedichte und Übersetzungen.* Offenbach am Main: André, 1882.

Music: Manuscript reproduced in Kalbeck's biography of Brahms, vol. III, page 526. *Fünf Lieder für eine tiefe Stimme,* Opus 94, No.4. Berlin: Simrock, 1884. Original key: D.

Sapphische Ode

H. Schmidt

Johannes Brahms
(Range: C4 – F5)

Ro - sen brach ich nachts mir am dunk - len Ha - ge; sü - ßer hauch - ten Duft sie, als je___ am Ta - ge; doch ver - streu - ten reich die be - weg - ten

ⓐ "Rather slowly." Suggestion: ♩ = ca. 80
ⓑ *Mezza voce* is usually a vocal marking, meaning "half voice." Here it means "softly," perhaps with soft pedal, for which the normal marking is *una corda* or *mit Verschiebung*.

Translation: At night I gathered roses that smelled sweeter than ever during the day, but the branches, being moved, scattered

© The double grace notes take part of the time of the preceding quarter. They should be sung as quickly and as late as possible, provided they are clear.

dew that made me wet. Also the fragrance of kisses moved me as never before, those which I gathered at night from your lips;

pflück - te;   doch auch   dir, be - wegt   im Ge-müt___ gleich

je - nen,   tau - ten die Trä -

nen!

but also on you, moved in your soul like the branches, tears welled up like dewdrops.

Wir wandelten
We Were Walking

Johannes Brahms (1833–1897)

viːr vandəltən wiːr tsvae tsuːzammən
1. Wir wandelten, wir zwei zusammen;
We strolled,   we two   together.

ıç vaːr zo: ʃtıll ʊnt du: zo: ʃtıllə
2. Ich war so still und du so stille;
I   was so quiet and you so quiet;

ıç gɛːbə   fiːl ʊm   tsu: ɛrfaːrən
3. Ich gäbe   viel, um   zu erfahren,
I   would-give much in-order to   learn

vas du: gədaxt ın jeːnəm fall
4. Was du gedacht in jenem Fall.
what you thought on that   occasion.

vas ıç gədaxt ʊnʔaosgəʃprɔxən
5. Was ich gedacht—unausgesprochen
What I   thought— unspoken

fɛrblaebə das nuːr ʔaenəs zaːk ıç
6. Verbleibe das! Nur Eines   sag' ich:
may-remain that! Only one-thing say I:

zo: ʃøːn waːr ʔalləs   vas ıç daxtə
7. So schön   war Alles,   was ich dachte,
So beautiful was everything that I   thought,

zo: hımmlıʃ haetər vaːr ɛs all
8. So himmlisch-heiter war es all.
so heavenly happy was it all.

ın maenəm haoptə diː gədaŋkən
9. In meinem Haupte die Gedanken,
In my   head   the thoughts,

ziː lɔøtətən viː gɔltnə glœkçən
10. Sie läuteten, wie goldne Glöckchen;
they rang   like golden little-bells;

zo: vʊndərzyːs zo: vʊndərliːplıç
11. So wundersüß,   so wunderlieblich
so wonder-sweet, so wonder-lovely

ıst ın der vɛlt kaen andrər hall
12. Ist in der Welt kein andrer Hall.
is in the world no   other   sound.

Georg Friedrich Daumer (1800–1875)
[geːɔrk friːdrıç daomər]

Poetic Background

"I would love to know what you were thinking as we walked together, but my thoughts were too beautiful ever to be told."

Including the poems of the waltzes called *Liebeslieder* and *Neue Liebeslieder*, Brahms set to music more than 60 of Daumer's poems. Kalbeck's biography tells a charming story about a time in 1872 when Brahms stopped in Würzburg specifically to meet Daumer. He was surprised to find that the poet of great love songs was a wrinkled little man, also surprised to learn that Daumer had never heard of him. In a joking manner Brahms alluded to the many beautiful lovers that Daumer had depicted in his poems. Laughing quietly, the old man called in a tiny old lady from the next room and introduced her: "This is the only woman I have ever loved— my wife."

The poem is said to be a translation from Magyar, the official language of Hungary.

Line 1: *wandelten* comes from *wandeln*, which means to walk slowly, without a particular goal.

Line 10: *läuteten*, Daumer wrote *lauteten*.

Musical Background

This song glows with warmth and color, perfectly capturing the tranquil mood of happy love from Daumer's poem. But analysis shows that the song is anything but simple and spontaneous. The pianist plays the principal melody first in the right hand with repeated tones above it to suggest the "golden bells" mentioned in line 10 of the poem. Starting two beats later the left hand plays the same melody in canon. After the voice enters, much of the same music is heard again in the piano. The second stanza begins normally (*Was ich gedacht. . .*), but after five measures the music moves in a completely unexpected direction. The new melody (*So schön war. . .*) has a hymn-like quality, but it is repeated with a new accompaniment that again suggests the "golden bells." The initial key returns with fragments of the initial melody accompanied by the treble bell sounds. Brahms prolongs the wonderful mood by repeating the words while the melody is permeated with the gentle two-note slurs that first appeared with the words *"was ich dachte. . ."*

Brahms worked hard to achieve the kind of technical perfection shown in *"Wir wandelten."* He set daily counterpoint problems for himself and untiringly studied music of earlier eras. Often he kept songs and other pieces in a state of incompleteness for years before either destroying them or giving them to his publisher. After a piece was engraved he made final changes during proofreading. He usually destroyed any sketches and manuscripts because he wanted the published version to have authority.

Brahms composed *"Wir wandelten"* during the spring and summer of 1884 in Vienna and Mürzzuschlag.

Sources

Text: *Polydora, ein weltpoetisches Liederbuch.* Frankfurt, 1855.
Music: *Vier Lieder*, Opus 96:2. Berlin: Simrock, 1886. Original key: D♭.

Wir wandelten

G. F. Daumer

Johannes Brahms
(Range: E♭4 – G♭5)

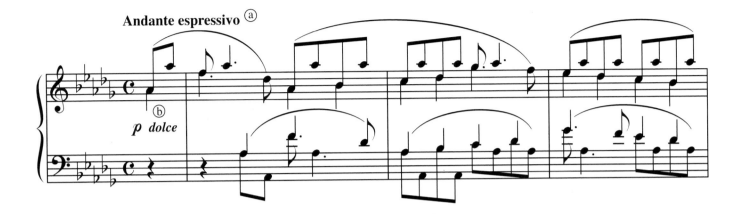

Wir   wan - del-ten,   wir

zwei   zu - sam - men;   ich____

ⓐ Suggestion: ♩ = ca. 80

ⓑ The lower notes in the right hand are to be sustained, as shown by the downward stems. The same applies to the upper notes in the left hand, shown by upward stems. These notes form a canon of the main melody.

ⓒ The canon between the hands begins again, as in m1.

Translation: We were walking, we two together. I

was so quiet and you were so quiet; I would give much to know what you were thinking at that time. What I was thinking—
may that remain unspoken! Just one thing I will say:

So beautiful were all my thoughts, so heavenly happy were they all. In my head the thoughts rang like little golden

ⓓ The melody of the voice is echoed by the inner notes of the offbeat chords.

ⓔ *Più dolce*, "sweeter," is an expression marking, perhaps also a slower tempo.

bells, more marvelously sweet and lovely than any other sound on earth.

Wie Melodien zieht es mir
Like Melodies that Pass

Johannes Brahms (1833–1897)

vi: melodi:ən tsi:t ʔɛs
1. Wie Melodien zieht es
Like melodies   moves it

mi:r laezə durç   den zɪnn
2. Mir leise durch den Sinn.
in-me softly through the mind.

vi: fry:lɪŋsblu:mən bly:t ʔɛs
3. Wie Frühlingsblumen blüht es
Like spring-flowers   blooms it

unt ʃve:pt vi: duft   dahɪn
4. Und schwebt wie Duft   dahin.
and drifts   like perfume around.

dɔx kɔmt das vɔrt unt fast ʔɛs
5. Doch kommt das Wort und fasst es
But   comes the word and seizes it

unt fy:rt ɛs fo:r das aok
6. Und führt es vor   das Aug',
and leads it before the eye;

vi: ne:bəlgrao ʔɛrblast ʔɛs
7. Wie Nebelgrau erblasst es
like fog-gray   pales   it

unt ʃvɪndət vi: aen haox
8. Und schwindet wie ein Hauch.
and disappears like a   breath.

unt dɛnnɔx   ru:t ɪm raemə
9. Und dennoch   ruht im Reime
And nevertheless remains in-the rhyme,

fɛrbɔrgən vo:l   aen duft
10. Verborgen wohl   ein Duft,
hidden   indeed, a   fragrance,

den mɪlt aos ʃtɪlləm kaemə
11. Den mild aus stillem Keime
which mildly from quiet   seed

aen fɔøçtəs ʔaogə ru:ft
12. Ein feuchtes Auge ruft.
a   moist   eye   calls.

Klaus Groth (1819–1899)
[klaos gro:t]

Poetic Background
"A formless feeling takes shape in a poem, and the person who reads it is mysteriously inspired to feel the same emotion as the poet had."

This poem is uncommonly abstract, an expression of poetic theory in poetic form. It tells how a vague poetic impulse in a poet's mind is communicated through written words to a sympathetic reader.

Most of Groth's writing was in *Plattdeutsch*, Low German; his poems in High German were published in *Hundert Blätter* (A Hundred Leaves), 1854. This is the last in a series of 13 short lyric poems called *"Klänge"* (Sounds).

Line 1: *Melodien* has a closed [e] vowel in the first syllable because it is borrowed from the French *"mélodie." Es* is never defined in this poem. *Something* moves through the poet's mind, producing a poem, but he does not define it more than to say "it" is *like* a fragrance.

Line 4: *dahin* usually means "away," but the fragrance does not "vanish" until line 8.

Lines 5 and 6: *Doch...Aug'* describes the act of putting the poetic feeling into written words.

Lines 9 and 10: *Und...Duft* is an inverted clause. A more normal word order might be: *"Und ein Duft ruht dennoch im Reime wohl verborgen."* ("And a fragrance remains nevertheless in the rhyme well hidden.")

Lines 11 and 12: *den* refers to *Duft*. In this clause the subject is *Auge*, the verb is *ruft*, and the object is *den*. Thus, "a moist eye" (metaphorically, a sensitive reader) "calls" forth a "fragrance" (metaphorically, the poetic inspiration, the undefined *es* from the first stanza). *Keime* is the dative of *der Keim*, a seed or shoot, metaphorically, a quiet source of mysterious growth.

Musical Background
Although Brahms never married, he had a number of almost-romantic friendships with musical women over the years. He wrote this song and the one that follows it in Opus 105, *"Immer leiser wird mein Schlummer,"* out of admiration for a beautiful alto singer, Hermine Spies. Both songs were written during a holiday in Thun, Switzerland, in August 1886, and Spies sang them there in a private performance at Brahms's house.

This mature work gives an example of Brahms's wonderful technique of strophic variation. Each of the three stanzas begins in the same way but modulates in a different direction. Because of the abstract and concentrated nature of the brief text, Brahms extends each stanza by inserting a brief interlude before repeating the final line or two of the stanza. In each case, the interlude (mm9–10, 22–23, and 36–37) is a descending melody in thirds that symbolizes the vaguely beautiful inspiration of which the poet speaks.

Brahms again used *alla breve* (¢) as a warning against too slow a tempo.

Sources
Text: *Hundert Blätter, Paralipomena zum Quickborn.* Hamburg: 1854. This version: *Sämtliche Werke*, vol. 5. Heide: Westholsteinische Verlagsanstalt Boyens, 1981.

Music: *Fünf Lieder für eine tiefere Stimme*, Opus 105, No. 1. Berlin: Simrock, 1888. Original key: A.

Wie Melodien zieht es mir

K. Groth

Johannes Brahms
(Range: C4 - G5)

ⓐ "Gently." Suggestion: 𝅗𝅥 = ca. 58

Translation: Something passes through my mind, blooms like a spring flower and vanishes like a fragrance.

Doch kommt das Wort und fasst es und

führt es vor das Aug', wie Ne - bel - grau er - blasst es und

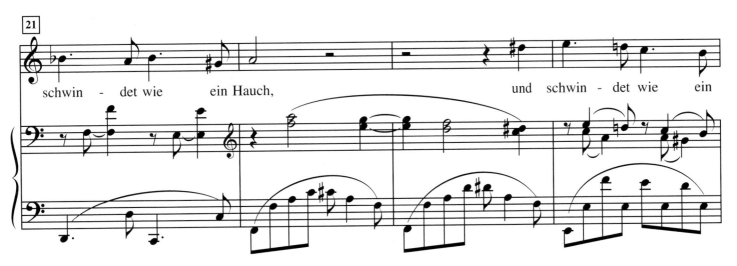

schwin - det wie ein Hauch, und schwin - det wie ein

Hauch. Und den - noch

But when the words come and seize it and make it visible, it loses its color and vanishes like a breath. And yet

ruht im Rei - me ver - bor - gen wohl ein Duft, den mild aus stil - lem

Kei - me ein feuch - tes Au - ge ruft, den

mild aus stil - lem Kei - me ein feuch - tes, ein feuch - tes

Au - ge ruft.

in the rhyme remains a hidden fragrance that can be awakened quietly by a tear-filled eye.

Der Gärtner
[der gɛrtnər]
The Gardener

Hugo Wolf (1860–1903)
[hu̱ːgo vɔlf]

ɑof iːrəm la̱ep.rœslaen
1. **Auf ihrem Leibrösslein,**
   On her   personal-little-horse,

zoː vaes viː der ʃneː
2. **So weiß wie der Schnee,**
   as white as   the snow,

diː ʃøːnstə prɪntsɛsɪn
3. **Die schönste Prinzessin**
   the loveliest princess

raet̯ dʊrç diː ʔalle̱ː
4. **Reit't durch die Allee.**
   rides down the avenue.

der veːk den   das rœslaen
5. **Der Weg, den   das Rösslein**
   The way on-which the little-horse

hɪnta̱ntsət zoː hɔlt
6. **Hintanzet   so   hold,**
   dances-away so   prettily,

der zant den ɪç ʃtrɔ̱øtə
7. **Der Sand, den ich streute,**
   the sand, that I   strewed,

er blɪŋkət viː gɔlt
8. **Er blinket wie Gold.**
   it sparkles like gold.

duː ro̱zənfarps hy̱ːtlaen
9. **Du rosenfarbs Hütlein,**
   You rose-colored little-hat,

voːl ʔɑof ʔʊnt voːl ʔap
10. **Wohl auf und wohl ab,**
    indeed up   and indeed down,

oː vɪrf aenə fe̱ːdər
11. **O wirf eine Feder**
    oh throw a   feather

fɛrʃto̱ːlən hɛra̱p
12. **Verstohlen herab!**
    surreptitiously downward!

ʊnt vɪlst duː dage̱ːgən
13. **Und willst du dagegen**
    And if-want you in-return

a̱enə bly̱ːtə fɔn miːr
14. **Eine Blüte von mir,**
    a   blossom from me,

nɪm tɑozənt fyːr a̱enə
15. **Nimm tausend für eine,**
    take a-thousand for one,

nɪm ʔallə dafy̱ːr
16. **Nimm alle dafür!**
    take all   for-it!

Eduard Mörike (1804–1875)
[e̱ːdŭart møːrɪkə]

Poetic Background
"I can never speak to the princess, but I serve her proudly and adore her from afar."

The singer's role in *"Der Gärtner"* is that of a humble worker on the grounds of a palace, thrilled by the sight of a beautiful princess who rides by without noticing him.

Line 1: the prefix *Leib-* means a servant, animal or thing for one person's use only.

Line 4: *reit't* is a contraction of *reitet. Die Allee* is a broad street, usually tree-lined. In this case, it is on the grounds of a palace.

Line 5: *der Sand* is necessary because the street is unpaved. The young gardener had the job of raking it clean to prepare for the princess's recreational ride.

Line 6: *rosenfarbs* is a contraction of *rosenfarbiges.*

Musical Background
Young Hugo Wolf composed more than 100 songs before a friend helped him find a publisher willing to bring out two collections, each containing six poems by various poets. Excited by this recognition, Wolf retired to a borrowed holiday home in Perchtoldsdorf, near Vienna. Isolated in the underheated house, he composed songs feverishly, as many as three in one day. He wrote 43 songs on Mörike texts between February and May, 1888, none during the summer and then ten more in autumn.

"Der Gärtner" was the 14th Mörike poem in order of composition, 17th in the published collection. It was composed on March 7, the same day as *"Elfenlied."* The first public performance of any of Wolf's songs had taken place in Vienna only five days before, adding to the young composer's enthusiasm.

The prancing rhythm of the piano part depicts the princess's snow-white horse. The rhythm and contours of the vocal melody fit the poem perfectly except for the first three words; apparently Wolf had to accept an uncomfortable beginning in order to get the melody he wanted for the rest of the song. Later, as he grew in confidence and skill, Wolf was meticulous about the relation between word stress and musical accent, and he no longer accepted compromises such as the one at the beginning of this song.

Like other great song composers, Wolf seldom wrote dynamics over the voice part. Working alone at the piano, he knew exactly how he wanted the piano part to be played, but perhaps he was less sure of the correct dynamic level to ask for from the singer. In studying the song the singer should locate the dynamic markings in the piano part and copy them above the voice part, modifying any that prove to be inappropriate.

Sources
Text: *Gedichte.* 1838.

Music: *Gedichte von Mörike,* No. 17. Vienna: Wetzler, 1889. Original key: D.

Der Gärtner

E. Mörike

Hugo Wolf
(Range: A4 – G5)

ⓐ "Lightly, gracefully." Suggestion: ♩. = ca. 80
ⓑ "Always staccato."

Translation: On her snow-white pet horse the pretty princess rides down the avenue.

Röss - lein hin - tan - zet so hold, der Sand,_____ den ich

streu - te, er blin - ket wie Gold.

Du ro - sen - farbs Hüt - lein, wohl auf und wohl

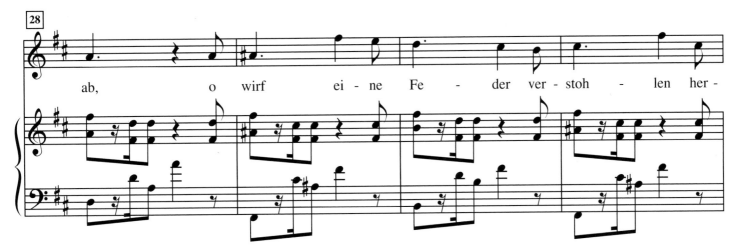

ab, o wirf ei - ne Fe - der ver - stoh - len her -

The little horse dances on the path I strewed with sand that sparkles like gold. Little pink hat, bouncing up and down, please let one of your feathers drift quietly

down to me! And if you want a blossom from me in return, take a thousand of them for one feather, take all my flowers
in trade!

Fußreise

[fuːsraͤezə]

Hiking

Hugo Wolf (1860–1903)

am frɪʃgəʃnɪtnən vandərʃtaːp
1. **Am frischgeschnittnen Wanderstab**
With-a freshly-cut walking-staff

vɛn ʔɪç ɪn der fryːə
2. **Wenn ich in der Frühe**
when I in the early-morning

zoː dʊrç vɛldər tsiːə
3. **So durch Wälder ziehe,**
thus through woods go,

hyːgəl ʔaof ʊnt ʔap
4. **Hügel auf und ab:**
hills up and down,

dan viːs føːklaͤen ɪm laobə
5. **Dann, wie's Vöglein im Laube**
then, as-the little-bird in-the greenery

zɪŋət ʊnt zɪç ryːrt
6. **Singet und sich rührt,**
sings and itself moves-around,

oːdər viː diː gɔltnə traobə
7. **Oder wie die goldne Traube**
or as the golden grape

vɔnnəgaͤestər ʃpyːrt
8. **Wonnegeister spürt**
joy-spirits feels

ɪn der eːrstən mɔrgənzɔnnə
9. **In der ersten Morgensonne:**
in the first morning-sun,

zoː fyːlt aox maen altər liːbər
10. **So fühlt auch mein alter, lieber**
so feels also my old, dear

aːdam hɛrpst ʔʊnt fryːlɪŋsfiːbər
11. **Adam Herbst- und Frühlingsfieber,**
Adam autumn and spring-fever,

gɔtbəhɛrtstə
12. **Gottbeherzte,**
God-inspired,

niː fɛrʃɛrtstə
13. **Nie verscherzte,**
never forfeited,

eːrstlɪŋs paradiːzəsvɔnnə
14. **Erstlings-Paradieseswonne.**
firstlings' paradise joy.

alzoː bɪst duː nɪçt zoː ʃlɪm ʔoː altər
15. **Also bist du nicht so schlimm, o alter**
So, are you not so bad, oh old

aːdam viː diː ʃtrɛŋən leːrər zaːgən
16. **Adam, wie die strengen Lehrer sagen;**
Adam, as the strict teachers say;

liːpst ʊnt loːpst duː ɪmmər dɔx
17. **Liebst und lobst du immer doch,**
love and praise you always indeed,

zɪŋst ʊnt praͤezəst ʔɪmmər nɔx
18. **Singst und preisest immer noch,**
you-sing and praise even yet,

viː an eːvɪç nɔøən ʃœpfʊŋstaːgən
19. **Wie an ewig neuen Schöpfungstagen,**
as on eternally new Creation-days,

daenən liːbən ʃœpfər ʊnt ʔɛrhaltər
20. **Deinen lieben Schöpfer und Erhalter!**
your dear Creator and Preserver!

mœçt ɛs diːzər geːbən
21. **Möcht' es dieser geben,**
May it like-this be,

ʊnt maen gantsəs leːbən
22. **Und mein ganzes Leben**
and my whole life

vɛːr ɪm laͤeçtən vandərʃvaͤesə
23. **Wär' im leichten Wanderschweiße**
were in-a light hiking-sweat

aenə zɔlçə mɔrgənraͤezə
24. **Eine solche Morgenreise.**
a such morning-journey.

Eduard Mörike (1804–1875)

Poetic Background

"On such a beautiful morning hike, my soul feels as happy and innocent as Adam in the Garden of Eden. I wish my whole life could be like this."

During the Romantic era, while poets were writing about their love of Nature, large numbers of people were losing contact with Nature by moving into industrially based cities. Hiking, instead of being most people's primary means of travel, became a healthful recreation and a means of re-connecting with the beauty of Nature. *Wandern*, for which "hiking" is an inadequate translation, became an important aspect of German culture and remains so today.

To grasp the meaning of Mörike's poem, one must recall the Creation story told in the Bible: how God created the first man and woman, Adam and Eve, who lived in the beautiful Garden of Eden until they offended God by following their own wishes instead of his. Some theologians, whom Mörike calls "the strict teachers," interpreted this story to mean that all humanity became tainted by an evilness that was inherited from Adam.

In this poem Mörike spoke to his innermost nature, called his "old Adam," and affirmed that it was "not so bad" after all. Surrounded by natural beauty, his soul still praised God as sincerely and innocently as did the "firstlings," Adam and Eve. Although Mörike was a clergyman, he rejected a theology that he considered to be overly negative.

The poem has an irregular form in three stanzas, each a complete sentence.

Line 3: *Wälder*, Mörike wrote *die Wälder*.

Line 5: *wie's* is a contraction of *wie das*. *Vöglein*, Mörike wrote *Vögelein*.

Line 10: *fühlt*, following a series of subordinate clauses, is the main verb of the sentence; its subject is *Adam* in line 11.

Line 13: *nie verscherzte*, literally "never joked-away," or "never forfeited in a foolish wager." Mörike's thought is that humanity has not irrevocably lost its blessed state.

Line 14: *Wonne* is equated by Mörike with the "spring fever" in line 11.

Line 20: *Schöpfer* is the object of the four verbs in lines 17 and 18.

Line 23: *Wanderschweiße*, an unpoetic concept in English, serves as evidence of the different concept and status of hiking in German culture.

Musical Background

Wolf wrote *Fußreise* on March 21, 1888, in the borrowed summer home where he was staying alone in Perchtoldsdorf. On the same day he wrote to his friend, Edmund Lang: "I retract my statement that '*Erstes Liebeslied eines Mädchens*' is my best, for what I wrote this morning is a million times better. . ."

He was composing every day in a fever of enthusiasm. "*Fußreise*" was the 23rd Mörike song in order of composition, the tenth in order of publication.

When Wolf accompanied a song in public, he liked to read the poem aloud to the audience and to expound on it before the singer sang it. He probably read a poem aloud to himself many times before composing it. This poem certainly has a complex grammatical structure that required careful planning for the music to flow naturally. The singer must also read the poem carefully to sense where words that form idea groups must be sung in one breath.

The song begins with a robust mezzo forte then becomes momentarily quiet (m. 17), as the poet listens to bird songs, then swells again to the first dynamic climax (m. 25). Throughout the song Wolf continued to give dynamic markings in the piano part that the singer must also observe.

Sources

Text: *Gedichte*, 1838.

Music: Music: *Gedichte von Mörike*, No. 10. Vienna: Wetzler, 1889. Original key: D Major.

Fußreise
E. Mörike

Hugo Wolf
(Range: E4 – G5)

ⓐ "Rather animated." Suggestion: ♩ = ca. 120

ⓑ Most hands cannot play the chord in m1, beats 2 and 3, without rolling it, which would be inappropriate for the character of the song. Do not roll the chord. Other options: (1) Omit the lower C, which is a doubled tone; (2) Take the B♭ with the left hand; (3) Play the B♭ an octave higher, where the fourth finger reaches it easily.

Translation: When I go out in early morning with a freshly cut staff in my hand,

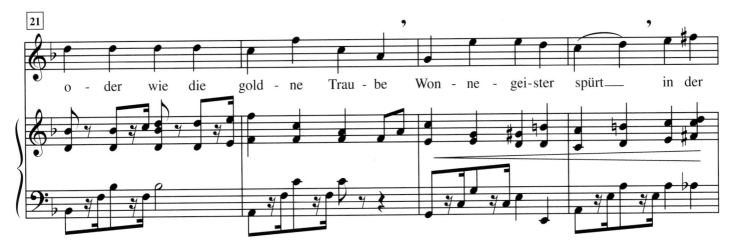

walking through forests, up and down hills, then, just as the little birds are singing and flying about, or as the golden grapes sense their juices rising in the

er - sten Mor - gen - son - ne:

So fühlt auch mein_ al - ter, lie - ber

A - dam Herbst und Früh - lings - fie - ber, gott - be - herz - te, nie ver - scherz - te

Erst - lings— Pa - ra - die - ses - won - ne.

first morning sunlight, then even my dear old Adam-nature feels autumn fever and spring fever, the joy, God-inspired and never given up, that the first created ones knew in Paradise.

etwas ruhiger ©

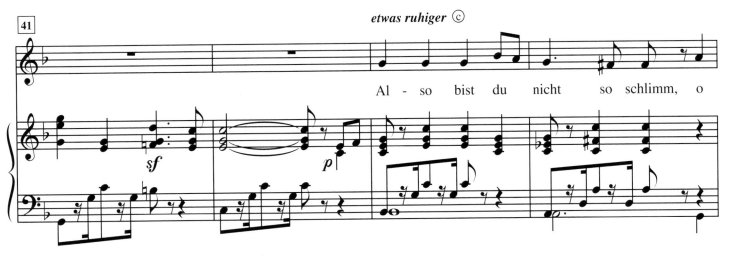

Al - so bist du nicht so schlimm, o

al - ter A - dam, wie die stren - gen Leh - rer sa - gen;

Liebst und lobst du im - mer doch,

© "More tranquilly." Suggestion: Keep the same tempo, but with smoother delivery.

So you are not as bad, old Adam, as the strict teachers say; you love and exalt God,

singst und prei-sest im-mer noch, wie an e-wig neu-en Schöp-fungs-

ta-gen, dei-nen lie-ben Schö-pfer

und___ Er - hal - ter!

you sing and praise Him even now, the same as on eternally new days of Creation, praise your dear Creator and Savior!

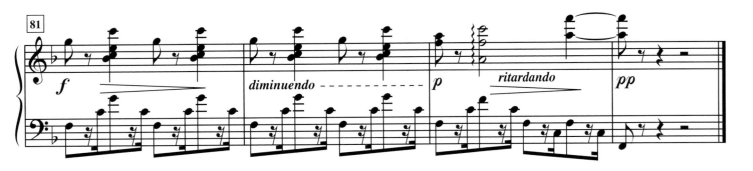

If only it could always be like this, and my whole life could be just like the gentle exertion of a morning hike.

Das verlassene Mägdlein
[das fɛrlasənə mɛːktlaen]
The Abandoned Maid

Hugo Wolf (1860–1903)

fryː van di hɛːnə krɛːn
1. Früh, wann die Hähne krähn,
Early, when the roosters crow,

eː di ʃtɛrnlaen ʃvɪndən
2. Eh' die Sternlein schwinden,
before the little-stars disappear,

mʊs ɪç am hɛːrdə ʃteːn
3. Muss ich am Herde stehn,
must I at-the hearth be,

mʊs fɔøər tsyndən
4. Muss Feuer zünden.
must fire light.

ʃøːn ɪst der flamən ʃaen
5. Schön ist der Flammen Schein,
Beautiful is the flames' light,

ɛs ʃprɪŋən di fʊŋkən
6. Es springen die Funken;
there leap the sparks;

ɪç ʃaoə zoː daraen
7. Ich schaue so darein,
I look so into-them,

ɪn laet fɛrzʊŋkən
8. In Leid versunken.
in sorrow sunk.

plœtslɪç da kɔmt ɛs miːr
9. Plötzlich, da kommt es mir,
suddenly, there comes it to-me,

trɔøloːzər knaːbə
10. Treuloser Knabe,
faithless boy,

das ɪç di: naxt fɔn diːr
11. Dass ich die Nacht von dir
that I the night of you

gətrɔømət haːbə
12. Geträumet habe.
dreamed have.

trɛːnə ʔaof trɛːnə dan
13. Träne auf Träne dann
Tear upon tear then

ʃtyrtsət hɛrniːdər
14. Stürzet hernieder;
stumbles downward;

zoː kɔmt der taːk hɛran
15. So kommt der Tag heran—
so comes the day toward-me—

oː gɪŋ eːr viːdər
16. O ging' er wieder!
oh, would-go it again!

Eduard Mörike (1804–1875)

Poetic Background
"I thought he loved me, but I was wrong. The day ahead will be one of work and silent misery."

Into a few lines of verse Mörike has put a human tragedy that has played itself out in many homes. The *Mägdlein* is a house-servant, a poor girl who left home in her early teens to work for a well to do family. A young son of the family declared his love for her and seduced her, but now he has gone away, perhaps to the university. She is alone in a life of drudgery, tormented by dreams about him and knowing that if her employer learns what has happened, she will be driven out of the house.

Mörike cast the poem in four four-line stanzas. Written in the late 1820s, it first appeared without a title in the novel *Maler Nolten* (Painter Nolten, 1832). There, the painter is awakened early in the morning by a serving girl singing this song, which in that context seems like a folk song. She is unknown to him, but the sound of her voice moves him to tears.

Line 2: *schwinden*, Mörike wrote *verschwinden*, same meaning.

Line 5: *Feuer zünden*; on cold mornings the maid must rise ahead of everyone else and re-light the fireplaces to warm the house.

Line 7: *darein*, Mörike wrote, *drein*.

Line 11: *die Nacht*, during the night.

Line 15: *heran*, as in older poetry and in some regional pronunciations, is sung with a long [aː].

Musical Background
Wolf wrote "*Das verlassene Mägdlein*" on March 24, 1888, in the borrowed summer home where he was staying alone in Perchtoldsdorf. It was the 26th Mörike song in order of composition, the seventh in the published volume.

'*Das verlassene Mägdlein*' was already an admirable song by Robert Schumann (Opus 64, No. 2, 1847); Wolf called it "heavenly." He usually avoided using any poem that had been set to music well by another composer. In this case, as he wrote to a friend three days later, Wolf felt that he was seized by the magic of the poem and composed the song without having meant to do so, almost against his own will. Wolf's thorough knowledge of the prior song is shown by the fact that he made the same text changes in lines 2 and 7 as Schumann had made.

At the beginning, the piano's thin chords are an image of coldness; their rhythm is the same (long-short-short) as the rhythm at the beginning of Schubert's "*Der Tod und das Mädchen.*"

The voice enters high, pianissimo, as the sad girl holds her feelings in and tries to deny them. Except for a slight crescendo to the word "*Funken,*" the first eight lines of the poem are sung pianissimo. And yet the persistent use of augmented triads produces uneasiness. At "*plötzlich*" her anger bursts out as the boy's image unexpectedly flashes into her mind. With difficulty she controls herself and returns, weeping, to her work.

A measure of rest (m44) reflects her unwillingness to face the coming day. But there is no ritard. The "*o*" expresses her wish for the day to pass quickly, but her work does not leave any time for sentimentality.

Sources
Text: *Gedichte.* 1838.

Music: *Gedichte von Mörike*, No. 7. Vienna: Wetzler, 1889. Original key: A minor.

Das verlassene Mägdlein

E. Mörike

Hugo Wolf

(Range: E4 – F5)

Langsam ⓐ

pp

Früh, wann die

Häh - ne krähn, eh' die Stern-lein schwin-den, muss ich am Her - de stehn,

muss Feu-er zün-den.

Schön ist der

ⓐ "Slowly." Suggestion: ♩ = ca. 44

Translation: Early, when the roosters crow and before the stars disappear, I have to be at the hearth and light the fire.
Beautiful is the

Flam - men Schein,   es sprin-gen die Fun - ken;   ich schau - e

so da - rein,   in Leid ver - sun - ken.

etwas lebhafter ⓑ

Plötz - lich,   da

etwas ruhiger ⓒ

kommt es mir,   treu - lo - ser Kna - be,   dass ich die

ⓑ "Somewhat quicker." Suggestion: ♩ = ca. 54

ⓒ "Somewhat slower." Suggestion: ♩ = ca. 50

firelight and the leaping sparks; I gaze at them, sunk in sorrow. Suddenly it occurs to me, faithless boy, that I

ⓓ "As at the beginning." Suggestion: ♩ = ca. 44

dreamt of you during the night. Tears upon tears fall down my cheeks. That's how the day begins. If only it would go away again!

Gesang Weyla's

[gəzaŋ vaelas]
Weyla's Song

Hugo Wolf (1860–1903)

duː bɪst ɔrpliːt maen lant
1. Du bist Orplid, mein Land!
You are Orplid, my land!

das fɛrnə lɔøçtət
2. Das ferne leuchtet;
which distant gleams;

fɔm meːrə dampfət daen bəzɔnntər ʃtrant
3. Vom Meere dampfet dein besonnter Strand
from-the sea steams your sunlit beach

den neːbəl zoː der gœtər vaŋə fɔøçtət
4. Den Nebel, so der Götter Wange feuchtet.
the mist, so the gods' cheek moistens.

uːrʔaltə vasər ʃtaegən
5. Uralte Wasser steigen
Primeval waters climb

fɛrjʏŋt ʊm daenə hʏftən kɪnt
6. Verjüngt um deine Hüften, Kind!
rejuvenated around your hips, child!

foːr daenər gɔthaet bɔøgən
7. Vor deiner Gottheit beugen
Before your divinity bow

zɪç køːnɪgə diː daenə vɛrtər zint
8. Sich Könige, die deine Wärter sind.
themselves kings, who your attendants are.

Eduard Mörike (1804–1875)

Poetic Background

"I call you into being and hail you, land of my dreams!"

Weyla is an imaginary bard, singing to an ideal island, both pure fantasies from the minds of Mörike and one or two of his fellow students at Tübingen. Orplid is mentioned only in Mörike's poetry and nowhere else in literature.

Lines 3 and 4 seem to say: the warmth of the sunny beach causes the sea water to steam up into mist and thus to moisten the "cheeks of the gods," a metaphor for the hills or cliffs that rise behind the beach.

Line 6: *verjüngt*, the island has such magical powers that "age-old waters" feel drawn there to become young again. Weyla calls the island *"Kind"* out of affection.

Lines 7 and 8: *beugen sich* is a reflexive verb. Despite the line ending, there must be no breath taken between the two words.

Musical Background

In October, 1888, Wolf was in Unterach, a scenic lakeside town in the Salzkammergut, as a guest of the Eckstein family. Wolf wrote *"Gesang Weyla's"* on October 9; it was the 50th Mörike song in order of composition, the 46th in the published volume.

Friedrich Eckstein was a well to do amateur musician who often allowed Wolf in Vienna to use his piano and his library. It was Eckstein who found a publisher for Wolf and guaranteed to make up any financial losses for the first books of songs. (So far as is known, Eckstein did not ever have to pay.)

Throughout *"Weyla's Song"* the piano takes the role of her harp. All chords are rolled before the beat; for example, in measure 2 the word *Du* is simultaneous with the highest note of the chord, not with the bass note. Only with the emotional word *"Kind"* does Wolf give the pianist a bit of melody to play. The vocal line contains wonderful examples of Wolf's rhythmic subtlety, beginning with the first two words. Both are important, so the first is on a downbeat and the second is syncopated. Syncopation is used in measures 7–10 to solve other problems of word stress in a masterful and original way.

Sources

Text: *Gedichte.* 1838.

Music: *Gedichte von Mörike,* No. 46. Vienna: Wetzler, 1889. Original key: D♭.

Gesang Weyla's

E. Mörike

Hugo Wolf
(Range: E♭4 – G5)

ⓐ "Slowly and solemnly." Suggestion: ♩ = ca. 60. The highest note of each chord is on the beat.

Translation: You are Orplid, my land, gleaming far away! Your sunny beach turns the sea to mist, and thus moistens

-ge feuch - tet. Ur - al - te Was - ser stei -

-gen ver - jüngt um dei - ne Hüf - ten, Kind!

Vor dei - ner Gott - heit beu - gen sich

Kö - ni - ge, die dei - ne Wär - ter sind.

the cheeks of gods. Primeval waters are rejuvenated as they wash your sides, my child! Your divinity is revered by kings, who are your attendants.

Anakreon's Grab

[anɑːkreɔns grɑːp]

Anacreon's Grave

Hugo Wolf (1860–1903)

   voː   diː roːzə hiːr blyːt   voː   reːbən ʊm   lɔrbeːr zɪç   ʃlɪŋən
1. Wo   die   Rose hier blüht, wo   Reben um   Lorbeer sich   schlingen,
   Where the rose   here blooms, where grapes around laurel   themselves wind,

   voː   das tʊrtəlçən lɔkt voː   zɪç das grɪlçən ʔɛrgœtst
2. Wo   das Turtelchen lockt, wo   sich das Grillchen ergötzt,
   where the turtledove   calls, where itself the cricket   enjoys,

   vɛlç aen grɑːp ɪst hiːr das allə gœtər mɪt leːbən
3. Welch ein Grab ist hier, das alle Götter mit Leben
   what   a   grave is here, that all   gods   with life

   ʃøːn   bəpflantst ʊnt gətsiːrt   ɛs ɪst anɑːkreːɔns ruː
4. Schön   bepflanzt und geziert? Es ist Anakreon's Ruh.
   beautifully planted   and decorated? It is Anacreon's rest.

   fryːlɪŋ   zɔmmər ʊnt hɛrpst gənɔs der glʏklɪçə dɪçtər
5. Frühling, Sommer und Herbst genoss der glückliche Dichter;
   Spring,   summer and autumn enjoyed the happy   poet;

   foːr dem vɪntər hat iːn ɛntlɪç der hyːgəl gəʃʏtst
6. Vor dem Winter hat ihn endlich der Hügel geschützt.
   from the winter has him finally the hill   protected.

Johann Wolfgang von Goethe (1749–1832)

Poetic Background

"We remember a happy poet with affection and marvel that Nature also shows regard for him."

Anacreon (582?–485? B.C.E.) is revered as a great lyric poet of ancient Greece, whose larger poems have all been lost. Some fragments survive because they were admired and quoted by later writers; they all celebrate the enjoyment of love and wine. (The tune of the American national anthem, "The Star-Spangled Banner," was originally an English drinking song that began "To Anacreon in heaven our voices we raise. . .")

In *"Anakreon's Grab"* Goethe imagined finding a tomb that was forgotten by humankind but still honored by the gods of nature. He used hexameter (six stresses per line) to give the poem a classical feeling and placed it in a collection entitled *"Antiker Form sich nähernd"* (approaching antique form).

Line 1: *Reben um Lorbeer. . .*, grapevines, symbolizing wine, are twining themselves around laurel trees, which symbolize poetic excellence. At the classical Olympic games the outstanding poet was crowned with laurel.

Line 2: *ergötzt*, Goethe wrote an older form, *ergetzt*.

Line 6: *Winter*, symbolizing old age, is the misfortune from which the poet is protected by the *Hügel*, the mound of earth over his grave.

Musical Background

At the end of summer, 1888, Wolf composed a group of Eichendorff settings and a few more Mörike poems while he was still a guest of the Ecksteins (see the commentary to *"Gesang Weyla's"*). Back home in Vienna, he turned his attention to Goethe. *"Anakreon's Grab"* was written on November 4, 1888 (and orchestrated in the early 1890s). Wolf wrote 50 Goethe songs in less than four months and later added one more to the collection of *Gedichte von Goethe*. *"Anakreons Grab"* was sixth to be composed and 29th in the published collection.

The mood is one of comfort, not of mourning. The scene is calm and lovely, and the memories of Anacreon are happy ones. The strongest note in the song is mezzo forte.

The music that underlies the first three phrases of the poem returns at m15; because the vocal line is completely new, the singer may not realize that the piano part is the same in mm3–5 and 15–17.

The great accompanist Gerald Moore wrote his advice for interpreting this song phrase by phrase, with far more detail than can be given here. (*Singer and Accompanist*. New York: Macmillan, 1954.) He rightly advises that the subtle syncopations in mm8–9 should not be accented, but disguised by calm legato singing.

Sources

Text: written about 1785. *Antiker Form sich nähernd*, *Werke*, vol 1, p. 358. Berlin: Tempel Verlag, 1959.

Music: *Gedichte von Goethe*. Vienna: C. Lacom, 1890. Original key: D.

Anakreon's Grab

J. W. von Goethe

Hugo Wolf
(Range: E4 – E5)

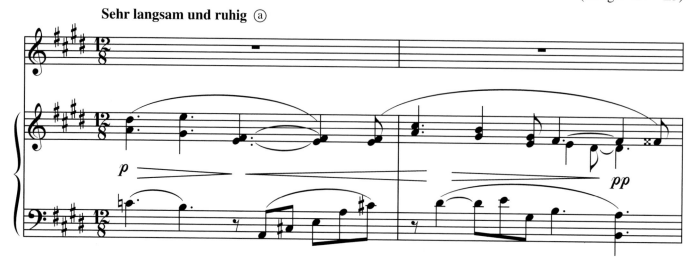

Wo die Ro - se hier blüht,_____ wo Re - ben um Lor-beer sich schlin - gen,

wo das Tur - tel-chen lockt,_____ wo sich das Grill-chen er - götzt,_____

ⓐ "Very slowly and calmly." Suggestion: ♪ = ca. 96
ⓑ "Gently."
ⓒ "Very gently."

Translation: Here where roses are blooming, where grapes and laurel twine, where turtledoves and crickets make their happy noises,

welch ein Grab ist hier, das__ al - le Göt - ter mit Le -

- ben schön be - pflanzt__ und ge - ziert?__

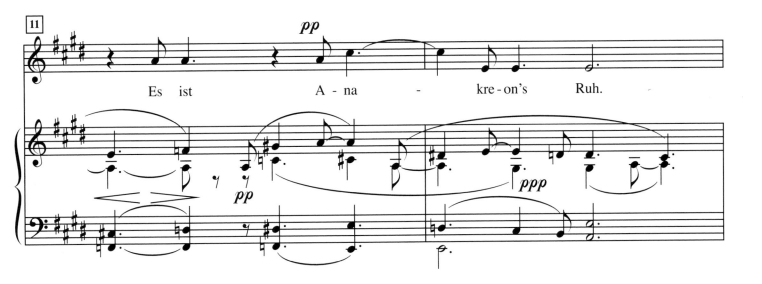

Es ist A - na - kre - on's Ruh.

what tomb is this, that all of the gods have adorned so beautifully with living things? It is the resting place of Anacreon.

Früh-ling, Som-mer und Herbst ge-noss____ der glück-li-che Dich-ter;

vor dem Win-ter hat ihn end - lich der Hü-gel ge-schützt.

ⓓ "Dying away."

The happy poet enjoyed spring, summer and autumn; now that it is winter, a mound of earth protects him.

In dem Schatten meiner Locken

In the Shade of My Locks

Hugo Wolf (1860–1903)

ɪn dem ʃatən   maenər lɔkən
1. In dem Schatten meiner Locken
In the shade   of my   locks

ʃliːf   miːr   maen gəliːptər ʔaen
2. Schlief mir   mein Geliebter ein.
slept   for-me my   beloved   in (went to sleep).

vɛk   ɪç iːn nuːn ʔɑof ax naen
3. Weck' ich ihn nun auf?—Ach nein!
Wake I   him now up?— Ah, no!

zɔrklɪç ʃtrɛːlt ɪç maenə krɑozən
4. Sorglich strählt' ich meine krausen
Carefully combed I   my   frizzy

lɔkən tɛːklɪç ɪn der fryːə
5. Locken täglich in der Frühe,
locks   daily   in the morning,

dɔx ʊmzɔnst ɪst maenə myːə
6. Doch umsonst ist meine Mühe,
but vain   is my   effort,

vael   diː vɪndə ziː tsɛrtsɑozən
7. Weil   die Winde sie   zerzausen.
because the winds them tousle.

lɔkənʃatən   vɪndəszɑozən
8. Lockenschatten, Windessausen
Hair-shadows,   wind's-whistle

ʃlɛːfərtən den liːpstən ʔaen
9. Schläferten den Liebsten ein.
slept   the beloved in (put him to sleep).

10. Weck' ich ihn nun auf? — Ach nein!

høːrən mʊs ɪç viː ʔiːn grɛːmə
11. Hören muss ich, wie ihn gräme,
Hear must I,   how he   suffers,

das er ʃmaxtət   ʃoːn zoː laŋə
12. Daß er schmachtet schon so lange,
that he languishes already so long,

das iːm   leːbən geːp   ʊnt neːmə
13. Daß ihm   Leben geb'   und nehme
that to-him life   would-give and take

diːzə maenə brɑonə vaŋə
14. Diese meine braune Wange.
this my   brown cheek.

ʊnt er nɛnt mɪç zaenə ʃlaŋə
15. Und er nennt mich seine Schlange,
And he calls me   his   snake,

ʊnt dɔx ʃliːf eːr bae miːr ʔaen
16. Und doch schlief er bei mir ein.
and yet slept   he by me   in (went to sleep).

17. Weck' ich ihn nun auf?—Ach nein!

Anonymous Spanish, translated by Paul Heyse.
[pɑol haezə]

Poetic Background

"I love this man who fell asleep beside me, but I'll let him sleep a little longer, anyway."

Paul Heyse, a leading writer of his time, collaborated with Emmanuel Geibel to make German translations of a collection of Spanish lyrics, calling it a *Spanish Songbook*. Mostly anonymous, the poems cover a wide range of themes, both sacred and secular.

This poem is frankly erotic; the woman and the sleeping man have been making love, although she says it is the wind that tousled her hair. And they will make love again, because she knows that as soon as he wakes he will start over with his love talk. The word *"Muss"* in line 11 does not mean that the necessity would be unpleasant. She is proud of her man and his passion, but she pretends to complain about his heated affirmations of his love. The whole poem might be a rehearsal for the gossip she will share with her friends the next day.

Line 7: *zerzausen* is shown incorrectly in the Peters edition and others as *zersausen*.

Line 15: *Schlange* might imply treachery, but is probably amorous. She is agile, and she has bitten him, either figuratively or physically.

The original Spanish poem ends with the question, "Shall I waken him or not?"

A la sombra de mis cabellos
mi querido se adurmió:
¿si le recordaré ó no?

Peinaba yo mis cabellos
con cuidado cada dia,
y el viento los esparcia
revolviéndose con ellos,
y á su suplo y sombra de ellos
mi querido se adurmió:
¿si le recordaré ó no?

Diceme que le da pena
el ser en extremo ingrata,
que le da vida y le mata
esta mi color morena,
y llamandome sirena
él junto á mí se adurmió:
¿si le recordaré ó no?

Musical Background

To compose the *Spanish Songbook,* Wolf returned to the place where he had written the Mörike songs, the poorly heated but congenial summer house at Perchtoldsdorf. Between October 1889 and April 1890 he composed ten sacred songs and 34 secular ones. On November 17, 1889, he wrote this song, the thirteenth in order of composition and second among the published secular songs.

Wolf later orchestrated the song and included it in his four-act comic opera, *Der Corregidor* (The Magistrate, 1895), where it is sung by Frasquita, the mezzo-soprano leading lady, in a mock seduction that leads to nothing.

The song opens with a lightly dancing rhythm that has a bit of Spanish flavor (although most songs in the collection have none at all). Notice that the first chord is detached, the second slurred to the third, and the remaining chords of measure 1 are treated as preparations for measure 2, which repeats the pattern. In most measures the first chord is detached from what follows, but nothing is staccato. Although they are to be played lightly, the parallel open fifths in the bass indicate the woman's peasant origin.

Brahms also used open fifths in the bass in his setting, called *"Spanisches Lied,"* Opus 6, No. 1. Adolf Jensen (1837–1879) also wrote a witty and distinctive setting.

Sources

Text: *Spanisches Liederbuch.* Berlin: Wilhelm Hertz, 1852.
   Music: *Spanisches Liederbuch.* Mainz: Schott, 1891.
Original key: B♭.

In dem Schatten meiner Locken

Spanish, translated by P. Heyse

Hugo Wolf
(Range: D4 – F5)

ⓐ "Light, gentle, not fast." Suggestion: ♩ = ca. 92

Translation: Shaded by my dark hair, my beloved went to sleep. Shall I wake him? Ah, no! Carefully

strählt' ich mei - ne krau - sen Lo - cken täg - lich in der Frü - he,

doch um-sonst ist mei-ne Mü - he, weil die Win - de sie zer-

zau - sen.

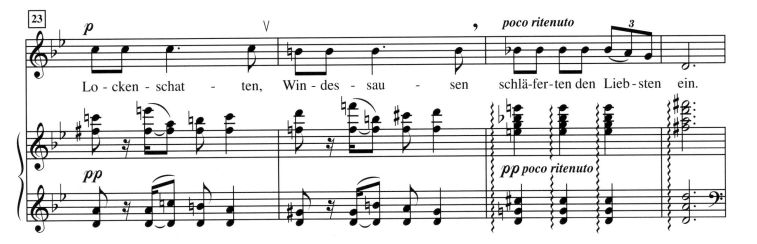

Lo - cken - schat - ten, Win - des - sau - sen schlä-fer-ten den Lieb-sten ein.

I combed my curly hair every morning, but my efforts are in vain because the wind tousles my hair again. The darkness of my hair, the sound of the wind put my lover to sleep.

Weck' ich ihn nun auf?____

Ach

nein!____   Hö - ren muss ich, wie ihn grä - me, dass er

schmach - tet schon so lan - ge, dass ihm Le - ben geb' und

neh-me die-se mei-ne brau - ne Wan - ge.

Shall I wake him? Ah, no! I would have to hear again about his suffering, how he has been languishing for so long, how his life depends on my brown cheeks.

And he calls me his snake, but he fell asleep beside me. Shall I wake him? Ah, no!

Auch kleine Dinge
Little Things, Too

Hugo Wolf (1860–1903)

aox klaenə dɪŋə kœnnən uns ʔɛnt.tsʏkən
1. Auch kleine Dinge können uns entzücken,
Also small   things can   us   delight,

aox klaenə dɪŋə kœnnən tɔøər   zaen
2. Auch kleine Dinge können teuer   sein.
Also small   things can   expensive be.

bədɛŋkt viː gɛrn viːr ʊns   mɪt pɛrlən ʃmʏkən
3. Bedenkt, wie gern wir uns   mit Perlen schmücken,
Consider how gladly we ourselves with pearls deck;

ziː veːrdən ʃveːr bətsɑːlt ʊnt zɪnt nuːr klaen
4. Sie werden schwer bezahlt und sind nur klein.
they are   heavily paid-for and are   only small.

bədɛŋkt viː klaen ɪst diː oliːvənfrʊxt
5. Bedenkt, wie klein ist die Olivenfrucht,
Consider how small is   the olive-fruit,

ʊnt vɪrt ʊm iːrə gyːtə   dɔx gəzuːxt
6. Und wird um ihre Güte   doch gesucht.
and it-is for its   goodness indeed sought.

dɛŋkt ʔan diː roːzə nuːr   viː klaen ziː ɪst
7. Denkt an   die Rose nur,   wie klein sie ist,
Think about the rose merely, how small it is,

ʊnt duftət dɔx zoː liːplɪç viː iːr vɪst
8. Und duftet   doch so lieblich, wie ihr wisst.
and perfumes indeed so lovely, as you know.

Anonymous Italian, translated by
Paul Heyse (1830–1914)

Poetic Background

"We love many small things; size is not proportional to love."

Paul Heyse gathered typical poems from several collections of Italian folk poetry published in the mid-1800s. This poem, like most of those that Wolf used, comes from Tuscany and is of a type called a *rispetto* (respect). *Rispetti* are love poems written in rhymed couplets, usually no more than twelve lines long. Many are adoring and idealistic, but many others are mocking or even insulting. For instance, one poem, *"Mein Liebster is so klein,"* mocks a short lover, while this poem lovingly praises small things. Since the Italian scholars who gathered these poems did not explain them, one can only guess whether *"Auch kleine Dinge"* is a compliment to a petite mistress or a consolation to an undersized lover.

Repetition is a frequent feature of *rispetti*, saying the same thing two or three times with slight changes in wording or word order. Heyse kept this feature when he translated the Italian original of *"Auch kleine Dinge."*

> *Le cose piccoline son pur belle!*
> *Le cose piccoline son pur care!*
> *Ponete mente come son le perle:*
> *Son piccoline, e si fanno pagare.*
> *Ponete mente come l' el' uliva:*
> *L'è piccolina, e di buon frutto mena.*
> *Ponete mente come l' è la rosa:*
> *L' è piccolina, e l' è tanto odorosa.*

Musical Background

Soon after Wolf completed his *Spanish Songbook* in April 1890, he composed *Alte Weisen* (old tunes), six poems by Gottfried Keller. In autumn 1890 he took up Heyse's Italian poems as his next project and composed seven of them. At that point his inspiration dried up, a problem that depressed him again and again as his life went on. Just over a year passed before he began to write again; he produced 15 more Italian songs in four weeks. *"Auch kleine Dinge"* was one of those, composed on December 9, 1891, in Döbling, at the suburban villa of Heinrich and Melanie Köchert. They were among Wolf's long-term supporters, and Melanie had been his lover for several years.

During the next three years Wolf had long dry periods; once he wrote to a friend that he could no sooner compose than begin suddenly to speak Chinese. In 1895 he completed his opera, *Der Corregidor* (The Magistrate). In 1896 the muse returned; in six weeks he composed another 24 Italian songs, resuming perfectly the style and manner that he had used in 1891.

The 46 songs of *Italian Songbook* are a high point in the art of the lied. By choosing *"Auch kleine Dinge"* to begin the published collection, Wolf invited listeners to accept these small songs as things of great value, just like pearls, olives and roses. A fine performance of the complete songbook requires three accomplished artists: a female and a male singer capable of finely shaped characterizations and a pianist capable of sensitive concentration throughout 46 songs. Considering the concentration required from the audience as well, it is usually preferable for one or two singers to perform a smaller selection of songs.

Thinking of smallness, Wolf begins *"Auch kleine Dinge"* with a four-note figure isolated high in the treble. The pianist must realize that the melody of the piano part is in the long syncopated tones in the left hand and remains there throughout the song. The singer's part is written mostly in stepwise motion with few leaps. After a series of repeated notes even a pitch change of a semitone seems important, as on the word *Güte*. Wolf also uses micro-phrases, as in mm12–13. Singer and pianist must aim for a performance that is both quiet and joyful, both intense and flexible.

Sources

Text: *Italienisches Liederbuch*. Berlin: Wilhelm Hertz, 1860.
  Music: *Italienisches Liederbuch*. Mainz: Schott, 1892.
Original key: A.

Auch kleine Dinge

Anonymous Italian, trans. P. Heyse

Hugo Wolf
(Range: E4 – F♯5)

ⓐ "Slow and very delicate." Suggestion: ♩ = ca. 54

Translation: Little things, too, can delight us; little things, too, can be dear. Just think how much we like to wear pearls; they are bought at a high price and are only little.

Be-denkt, wie klein ist die O - li - ven-frucht, und wird um ih - re Gü -

- te doch ge-sucht._ Denkt an die Ro - se nur, wie klein sie ist,

etwas breiter ⓑ
sehr zart   *a tempo*

und duf - tet doch so lieb - lich,   wie_ ihr__ wisst.

ⓑ "Somewhat broader" and "Very delicate."

Just think how small is an olive, and people seek it out for its goodness. Think about a rose, how small it is, and gives a lovely fragrance, as you know.

Die Nacht
Night

Richard Strauss (1864–1949)
[rɪçart ʃtraos]

ɑos   dem valdə trɪt   diː naxt
1. **Aus dem Walde tritt die Nacht,**
From the forest steps the night,

ɑos den bɔømən ʃlaeçt   ziː laezə
2. **Aus den Bäumen schleicht sie leise,**
from the trees   slips   it quietly,

ʃɑot zɪç ʊm ɪn   vaetəm kraezə
3. **Schaut sich um   in   weitem Kreise—**
looks itself around in-the wide   circle—

nuːn giːp ʔaxt
4. **Nun gib acht!**
now give attention!

allə lɪçtər   diːzər vɛlt
5. **Alle Lichter dieser Welt,**
All lights of-this world,

allə bluːmən allə farbən
6. **Alle Blumen, alle Farben**
all flowers, all colors

lœʃt   ziː ʔɑos ʊnt ʃtiːlt diː garbən
7. **Löscht   sie aus und stiehlt die Garben**
extinguishes it out and steals the sheaves

vɛk fɔm   fɛlt
8. **Weg vom   Feld.**
away from-the field.

alləs   nɪmt ziː vas   nuːr hɔlt
9. **Alles   nimmt sie, was   nur hold;**
Everything takes it that [is] only lovely,

nɪmt das zɪlbər vɛk dɛs   ʃtroːms
10. **Nimmt das Silber weg des   Stroms,**
takes the silver away of-the river,

nɪmt vɔm   kʊpfərdax dɛs doːms
11. **Nimmt vom   Kupferdach des Doms**
takes from-the copper-roof of-the cathedral

vɛk das gɔlt
12. **Weg das Gold.**
away the gold.

ɑosgəplyndərt ʃteːt der ʃtraox
13. **Ausgeplündert steht der Strauch—**
all-plundered is   the shrubbery—

rʏkə nɛːər zeːl an zeːlə
14. **Rücke näher, Seel' an Seele,**
move nearer, soul to soul,

oː diː naxt miːr baŋt   ziː ʃteːlə
15. **O die Nacht, mir bangt,   sie stehle**
oh, the night, I   am-afraid, it may-steal

dɪç miːr   ɑox
16. **Dich mir   auch.**
you from-me also.

Hermann von Gilm (1812–1864)
[hɛrman fɔn gɪlm]

Poetic Background

"As every beautiful thing fades at sunset, the thought comes to me that I may lose you, beloved."

Gilm's poems mostly remained unpublished until the year of his death. This one and *"Allerseelen"* were included in a group entitled *Letzte Blätter* (Last Leaves), implying that they were written near the end of Gilm's life. Married for the first time at 49, he was a father at 50 and died at 51. The facts of late love and fatherhood would explain a preoccupation with fear of loss.

Each of the poem's four stanzas has three longer lines and a short, three-syllable line. The rhyme scheme and trochaic meter are maintained with perfect consistency.

Line 4: *gibt*, Gilm used the old spelling *giebt*, a reminder of the long vowel.

Lines 10 and 11: *Stroms. . . Doms*, Gilm wrote *Stromes . . . Domes*.

Line 12: *Gold* is the appearance of the copper roof in the light of the setting sun.

Line 13: *ausgeplündert steht der Strauch* because darkness has robbed the flowers of their color.

Musical Background

Strauss composed 42 songs before he was introduced to Gilm's poetry by another composer, Ludwig Thuille. He completed this mature, and now famous song on August 11, 1885, when he was 21 years old and still living at home in Munich.

This song is an early example of the broad, *bel canto* melody for which Strauss is famous. Each of the four stanzas begins from the same rising scale-wise motive, but each develops differently. The fourth is longer than the others only because of its long note values.

Songs by Strauss have a different appearance from all other songs in this book because of the long slur markings used over many phrases to encourage legato singing. A slur marking may indicate where the composer recommended a breath, or it may indicate an expressive line that lasts longer than one breath. Such slur markings came into standard use in vocal editions in the first half of the 1900s, so that editors often added them to the works of composers who had not originally used them.

In addition to an expressive slur in m15, there is another slur present also. It is obviously not connecting two or more notes on one syllable, a melisma. It is a fourth kind of slur, a *portamento* that connects the two syllables *"die Gar-."* In this period it means that the voice quickly and lightly slides from one pitch to the other. Vocal composers rarely, but occasionally indicated *portamenti*; examples are found in songs by Alban Berg and Joseph Marx. In general, modern German singers avoid *portamenti*, but they were in use in decades just before and after 1900.

The pianist must observe the commas that Strauss placed at the end of m9 and m17.

Strauss stated that he had a tenor voice in mind for the Gilm songs. He dedicated them to the principal tenor of the Munich Court Opera, Heinrich Vogl (no relation to Vogl, the friend of Schubert).

Sources

Text: *Gedichte*. Leipzig: Philipp Reclam, jun., 1895.
   Music: *8 Lieder aus Letzte Blätter*, Opus 10, No. 3.
Munich: Aibl, 1885. Original key: D.

Die Nacht

H. von Gilm

Richard Strauss
(Range: C♯4 – G5)

ⓐ Suggestion: ♩ = ca. 62

ⓑ Regarding *portato* markings, which are found in the piano part throughout, Hermann Reutter taught that the notes are played with the damper pedal held down. This interpretation is probably valid generally for Romantic and post-Romantic music.

Translation: Out of the forest steps Night, slipping quietly from the trees, looking all around— now, beware! Night extinguishes all the world's lights, all flowers, all

colors, and it steals the sheaves of wheat from the fields. It takes away everything lovely, the silver ripple of the stream, the golden glow of the cathedral's dome. Plundered

steht der Strauch, rü - cke nä - her, Seel' an See -

le; o die Nacht, mir bangt, sie steh -

le dich mir auch.

of flowers are the shrubs— move closer to me, soul to soul. O, I fear that Night may steal you away from me, too.

Allerseelen
[ˈalərzeːlən]
All Souls' Day

Richard Strauss (1864–1949)

ʃtɛl ʔaof den tɪʃ diː duftəndən rezeːdən
1. Stell' auf den Tisch die duftenden Reseden,
  Place on the table the fragrant mignonettes,

diː lɛtstən roːtən ʔastərn traːk hɛrbae
2. Die letzten roten Astern trag' herbei,
  the last red asters bring here,

ont las ons viːdər fɔn der liːbə reːdən
3. Und lass uns wieder von der Liebe reden,
  and let us again of [-] love talk,

viː ʔaenst ɪm mae
4. Wie einst im Mai.
  as once in May.

giːp miːr diː hant das ɪç ziː haemlɪç drykə
5. Gib mir die Hand, dass ich sie heimlich drücke,
  Give me the hand, so-that I it secretly may-press,

ont vɛn mans ziːt miːr ɪst ɛs ʔaenərlae
6. Und wenn man's sieht, mir ist es einerlei;
  the if one-it sees, to-me is it all-the-same

giːp miːr nuːr ʔaenən daenər zyːsən blɪkə
7. Gib mir nur einen deiner süßen Blicke,
  give me only one of-your sweet glances,

8. Wie einst im Mai.

ɛs blyːt ont duftət hɔøt ʔaof jeːdəm graːbə
9. Es blüht und duftet heut' auf jedem Grabe,
  There blooms and perfumes today on every grave,

aen taːk ɪm jaːr ɪst jaː den toːtən frae
10. Ein Tag im Jahr ist ja den Toten frei;
  one day in-the year is indeed to-the dead free.

kɔm ʔan maen hɛrts das ɪç dɪç viːdər haːbə
11. Komm' an mein Herz, dass ich dich wieder habe,
  Come to my heart, so-that I you again have,

12. Wie einst im Mai.

  Hermann von Gilm (1812–1864)

Poetic Background
"Our love was long ago, but let us remember it, just for today."

All Souls' Day, November 2, is a holy day when Roman Catholics say special prayers for departed souls. Many Germans and Austrians who have moved away from home travel back for that day to decorate the graves of their parents.

All Souls' Day is the occasion for this song. Two persons who were in love years ago meet by accident. Each has gone an independent way; they are not thinking of becoming lovers again. Yet in this poem one asks the other to spend time, sitting together, talking about love and holding hands. They will

not even be alone— it does not matter if others see them. They will embrace just once, to say goodbye. (Lotte Lehmann interpreted the poem differently, but convincingly in *More Than Singing* [London: Boosey and Hawkes, 1946].)

Some singers have imagined that the beloved is dead, but the poem is filled with concrete details of a real meeting of two living persons. It seems clear that Gilm was writing about a true incident; he was in love several times before his late marriage.

Each of the three stanzas has three longer lines and a refrain, "As once in May."

Line 4: *Mai* symbolizes an earlier time of youth and love in a long past year, not the preceding May according to the calendar.

Line 9: *es blüht und duftet* because every grave is decorated with fragrant flowers. A later edition of the poem has *es blüht und funkelt* (sparkles) because on every grave there is an oil lamp or votive candle, and the cemetery will glow after sunset. It is not clear whether Gilm or Strauss made the word choice.

Line 10: *den Toten frei*, in the sense that on this day the dead are honored and forgiven for whatever they have done. In the same spirit, these former lovers honor their past love with forgiveness.

Musical Background
Strauss completed *"Allerseelen"* on October 31, 1885. It is remarkable that this song of mature love and nostalgia was convincingly composed by a 21-year-old.

At the outset the piano strongly establishes the tonic key and moves into a phrase with a broad, emotional sweep (m4–8), during which the voice slips in unobtrusively. Some of the same music returns at m27 as accompaniment to the voice (it would be interesting to know which was composed first, m1 or m27). When the voice reaches its highest tone, the pitch is the same one as at the climax of the piano introduction.

In m39 is an example of a portamento similar to the one in m15 of *"Die Nacht"* (discussed on page 199).

"Allerseelen" was recorded for the first time in 1903. A piano solo version was arranged by Max Reger for publication in 1904; many other arrangements followed. Strauss made a piano roll of the accompaniment around 1921.

Sources
Text: *Gedichte.* Leipzig: Philipp Reclam, jun., 1895.

  Music: *8 Lieder aus Letzte Blätter*, Opus 10, No. 8. Munich: Aibl, 1885. Original key: E♭.

Allerseelen

H. von Gilm

Richard Strauss
(Range: D4 – A♭5)

ⓐ Suggestion: ♩ = ca. 72

Translation: Put fragrant mignonettes on the table, bring in the last red asters, and let us talk about love,

as once in May. Give me your hand so that I can hold it secretly, and even if people see, I don't mind.

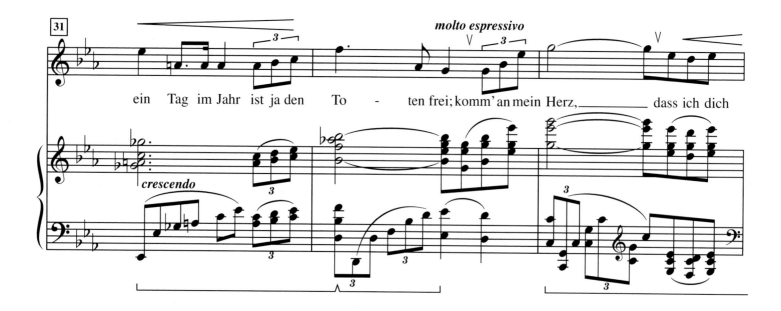

Give me just one of your sweet glances, as once in May. There are fragrant flowers today on every grave;

wie - der ha - be, wie einst im Mai,

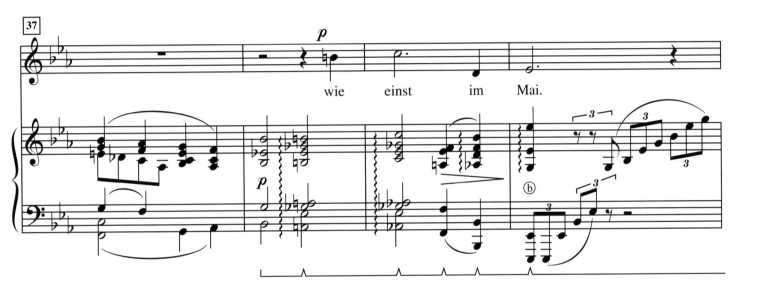

wie einst im Mai.

ⓑ The lowest note of the right hand chord must be played with the bass note, and the chord is arpeggiated quickly.
ⓒ The lowest note of the right hand is played with the bass note, and both hands arpeggiate slowly at the same time.

one day a year is devoted to the dead. Come and embrace me, so that I again possess you, as once in May.

All mein Gedanken, mein Herz und mein Sinn
All My Thoughts, My Heart and My Mind

Richard Strauss (1864–1949)

al maen gədaŋkən maen hɛrts ʊnt maen zɪn
1. All mein Gedanken, mein Herz und mein Sinn,
   All my   thoughts   my   heart and my   mind,

dɑː voː diː liːpstə   ɪst vandərn ziː hɪn
2. Da wo   die Liebste   ist, wandern sie hin.
   there where the most-loved is, go   they toward.

geːn iːrəs veːgəs trɔts maoər ʊnt toːr
3. Geh'n ihres Weges trotz   Mauer und Tor,
   go   their   way   despite wall   and gate,

dɑː hɛlt kaen riːgəl kaen grɑːbən nɪçt foːr
4. Da   hält kein Riegel, kein Graben nicht vor,
   there holds no   bar,   no   moat   not   in-the-way,

geːn viː diː føːgəlaen hoːx dʊrç diː lʊft
5. Geh'n wie die Vögelein   hoch durch die Luft,
   go   like the little-bird high through the air,

braoxən kaen brykən yːbər vasər ʊnt klʊft
6. Brauchen kein' Brücken über Wasser und Kluft,
   need   no   bridges over water   and ravine,

fɪndən das ʃtɛtlaen ʊnt fɪndən das haos
7. Finden das Städtlein und finden das Haus,
   find   the little-town and find   the house,

fɪndən iːr fɛnstər aos allən heraos
8. Finden ihr Fenster aus allen heraus,
   find   her window   from all   out,

ʊnt klɔpfən ʊnt ruːfən max   aof las ʊns aen
9. Und klopfen und rufen: "Mach' auf, lass uns ein,
   and knock   and call,   "Make   open, let   us   in,

viːr kɔmmən fɔm liːpstən ʊnt gryːsən dɪç faen
10. Wir kommen vom   Liebsten und grüßen dich fein."
   we   come   from-the most-loved and greet   you   nicely."

Felix Dahn (1834–1912)
[feːlɪks dɑːn]

Poetic Background

"I imagine that my thoughts fly to you like little birds and bring greetings from me."

Dahn wrote: "In the second issue of the newsletter of the Germanic Museum, 1853, I found the beginnings of many old folksongs listed. Inspired by their pithy expressions, I used them for simple songs. The continuation of all these songs is completely unknown to me. . ."

The museum referred to is the Germanisches Nationalmuseum in Nuremburg, founded in 1852 and devoted to folk arts. Dahn called his set of poems "Schlichte Weisen" (simple tunes), an attractive title that Strauss kept for his songs.

For this poem Dahn had only the first three words, "All mein Gedanken," for inspiration. The same words begin a song from the 1500s that Brahms included among his *Deutsche Volkslieder*.

Dahn used an unusual meter in the first four lines: / _ _ / _ _ / _ _ /, or three dactyls and a spondee. He varied the pattern with added syllables in the other lines.

Line 3: *geh'n* and all of the other verbs lack their subject, *sie*, to avoid weak syllables at the beginnings of lines.

Line 5: *Vögelein* as symbols of thoughts occured in Heine's *"Aus meinen großen Schmerzen"* (page 120).

Musical Background

When Strauss completed *"All mein Gedanken"* on February 12, 1889, he had nearly finished a three year contract as third conductor at the Munich Court Opera (now the Bavarian National Theater). He was a busy and ambitious young musician, and during this period he was composing his tone poem *Don Juan*. His songs show a fine understanding of the singing voice, and he was in love with soprano Pauline de Ahna, who later became his wife and performed often with him in public.

"All mein Gedanken" is a merry trifle, more diatonic than most songs by Strauss. There are humorous touches: the added beat for *"Liebste;"* the off-beat accent for *"ihr."* In measures 18–22 the voice is high like a bird's voice and quiet as if heard through the window. The unexpected cadenza on *"grüßen"* is preceded by a six-four chord, just like the cadenza of a piano concerto.

The composer Max Reger paid this song a double compliment: he arranged it for piano solo (1904) and he wrote his own setting of the text (1903–04).

Sources

Text: *Schlichte Weisen* (no. 18), in *Jugend-Gedichte (1848–1855)*, in *Sämtliche Werke poetischen Inhalts*, vol. 16. Leipzig: Breitkopf und Härtel, 1898?.

Music: *5 Lieder 'Schlichte Weisen,'* Opus 21, No. 1. Munich: Aibl, 1890. Original key: E.

All mein Gedanken, mein Herz und mein Sinn

F. Dahn

Richard Strauss
(Range: C♯4 – G♯5)

ⓐ Suggestion: ♩ = ca. 74

Translation: All my thoughts, my heart and my mind, wander off to where my sweetheart is. They make their way in spite of walls and gates, no bar or moat stops them. They go through the air up high, like birds,

they need no bridges over water or ravines. They find the little town and find the house, and seek out her window from all the others, and knock and call: "Open up, let us in! We come from your

sten   und grü   -   ßen dich

fein,   wir kom - men vom Lieb - sten und grü - ßen dich fein,   mach'

auf,   mach' auf,____ lass uns ein.

sweetheart and bring you greetings!"

Du meines Herzens Krönelein
You, the Little Crown of My Heart

Richard Strauss (1864–1949)

du: m<u>a</u>enəs h<u>ɛ</u>rtsəns krø:nəlaen du bɪst fɔn l<u>ʊ</u>otrəm g<u>ɔ</u>ldə
1. **Du meines Herzens Krönelein, du bist von lautrem Golde:**
You my   heart's   dear-crown, you are   of   pure   gold;

vɛn <u>a</u>ndərə dan<u>e</u>:bən zaen dan bɪst du: nɔx fi:l h<u>ɔ</u>ldə
2. **Wenn Andere daneben   sein, dann bist du noch viel holde.**
when other   beside-you are, then are you still much lovelier.

di: ʔ<u>a</u>ndərn tun zo: gɛrn gəʃ<u>ɔ</u>øt du: bɪst gɑ:r zanft ʊnt ʃt<u>ɪ</u>llə
3. **Die Andern tun so gern gescheut, du bist gar   sanft und stille;**
The others   do so   gladly bashful, you are   entirely gentle and quiet;

das j<u>e</u>:dəs hɛrts zɪç daen   ɛrfr<u>ɔ</u>øt daen glʏk   ɪsts nɪçt daen v<u>ɪ</u>llə
4. **Dass jedes Herz sich dein   erfreut, dein Glück   ist's, nicht dein Wille.**
that every   heart itself about-you rejoices, your good-fortune is-it, not   your will.

di: <u>a</u>ndərn zu:xən li:p ʊnt gʊnst mɪt‿t<u>ao</u>zənt f<u>a</u>lʃən v<u>ɔ</u>rtən
5. **Die Andern suchen Lieb' und Gunst mit tausend falschen Worten,**
The other   seek   love and favor with thousand lying   words,

du: <u>o</u>:nə   mʊnt ʊnt <u>ao</u>gənkʊnst bɪst ve:rt an <u>a</u>llən <u>ɔ</u>rtən
6. **Du, ohne   Mund-und Augenkunst, bist wert   an allen Orten.**
you, without mouth or eye-art,   are worthy in all   places.

du: bɪst als vi: di: ro:z ɪm   valt zi: vaes nɪçts fɔn i:rər bl<u>y</u>:tə
7. **Du bist, als wie die Ros' im   Wald: sie weiß nichts von ihrer Blüte,**
You are, as like the rose in-the woods: it knows nothing of its   bloom,

dɔx j<u>e</u>dəm   der for<u>y</u>:bərvalt ɛrfr<u>ɔ</u>øt zi: das gəm<u>y</u>:tə
8. **Doch jedem,   der vorüberwallt, erfreut sie das Gemüthe.**
but for-everyone who passes-by   gladdens it   the mood.

Felix Dahn (1834–1912)

Poetic Background

"You bring me joy without even knowing that you do so."

The background of Dahn's *Schlichte Weisen* is described in the commentary to *"All mein Gedanken"* (page 208).

This single stanza poem appears to have unusually long lines with seven stresses in each. Read aloud, it sounds more conventional, as if it had alternating lines of four and three stresses, all of them rhymed. For instance, *Krönelein* in the middle of line 1 rhymes with *sein* in line 2, and so on throughout.

Line 2: *noch viel holde* should read *holder*, but Dahn dropped the final *r* for the sake of the rhyme with *Golde*. A later edition had *erst viel holde,* but that is not an improvement.

Line 3: *tun* here expresses pretense. "They act shy" rather than "they are shy."

Line 4: *dass* stands for "The fact that. . ."

Line 6: *Mund- und Augenkunst* is itself an artful phrase that uses *Kunst* not in its primary meaning of art, but its secondary meaning of artificiality. The whole phrase means: flirtation with unnatural manipulation of the mouth and eyes. *An allen Orten* is often used to mean "in all circumstances."

Musical Background

Strauss completed this song on April 7, 1889, in Munich where he was a conductor at the opera.

Like the young person described in the poem, this song has more to offer than the listener at first realizes. Each of the poem's four couplets is set differently. A gentle, richly accompanied melody that stands for the beloved (mm1–2) is contrasted with a busier, staccato texture that stands for the flighty, superficial "others" (m5). Slurs and melismas are associated with the beloved, quick declamation with the others. The primary melody returns inconspicuously in m11 and m16 before its most important return in mm27–28. This coincides not with the beginning of the fourth couplet, where we expect it, but with the word *"nichts,"* which emphasizes the beloved's lack of self-awareness.

Another musical symbol of the beloved's innocence is the high tonic note in m2, first sung on the vowel [u], inevitably a head tone. It begins a downward octave arpeggio that occurs in the second and fourth phrases of the first couplet. When the primary melody returns, the arpeggio occurs twice in the third phrase of the couplet (mm24–26). The same high tone, sung on *"du,"* also occurs in the second phrase of the second couplet (m10) and in the third phrase of the third couplet (m20). With his prodigious mastery of tonal modulation, Strauss could manipulate these contrasting thematic ideas so that every idea of the poem has its appropriate music.

The brief piano postlude combines the downward arpeggio in the treble with a shy echo of the main melody in the bass.

The composer Max Reger paid this song a double compliment, as he did with *"All mein Gedanken"*: he arranged it for piano solo (1904) and he wrote his own setting of the text (1909).

Sources

Text: *Schlichte Weisen* (no. 13), in *Jugend-Gedichte (1848–1855)*, in *Sämtliche Werke poetischen Inhalts*, vol. 16. Leipzig: Breitkopf und Härtel, 1898?.

Music: *5 Lieder "Schlichte Weisen,"* Opus 21, No. 2. Munich: Aibl, 1890. Original key: G♭.

Du meines Herzens Krönelein

F. Dahn

Richard Strauss
(Range: D♭4 – G♭5)

ⓐ Suggestion: ♪ = ca. 76

Translation: You, the little crown of my heart, you are made of pure gold; when others are nearby, then you seem all the lovelier. The others like

to pretend they are shy, but you are simply gentle and quiet; that you make others glad is your good fortune, not by your will. The others seek to win love and favor with a thousand flatteries; you, without any artifice of word

Au - gen kunst, bist wert an al - len Or - ten.

Du bist, als wie die Ros' im Wald, sie weiß nichts_____ von ih - rer

Blü - the, doch je - dem, der vor - ü - ber - wallt, er -

freut_____ sie das Ge - mü - the.

or look, are worthy in every way. You are just like a rose in the forest: it is unaware of its bloom, but everyone who passes by is made happy by it.

Phonemes of German

IPA Symbols	Names of Symbols	Similar English Sounds
1. [iː] or [i]	Lower-Case I	mach<u>i</u>ne
2. [ɪ]	Small capital I	s<u>i</u>zzle
3. [eː] or [e]	Lower-Case E	cha<u>o</u>tic
4. [ɛː] or [ɛ]	Epsilon	r<u>e</u>d
5. [ɑː] or [a]	Lower-Case A	f<u>a</u>ther
6. [ə]	Schwa	shov<u>e</u>l
7. [uː] or [u]	Lower-Case U	tr<u>u</u>th
8. [ʊ]	Upsilon	p<u>u</u>sh
9. [oː] or [o]	Lower-Case O	<u>o</u>ceanic
10. [ɔ]	Open O	<u>ou</u>ght
11. [yː] or [y]	Lower-Case Y	(none)
12. [ʏ]	Small capital Y	(none)
13. [øː] or [ø]	Slashed O	(none)
14. [œ]	O-E Ligature	(none)
15. [m]	Lower-case M	<u>m</u>ime
16. [n]	Lower-case N	<u>n</u>oon
17. [ŋ]	Eng	si<u>ng</u>
18. [l]	Lower-case L	<u>l</u>augh
19. [r]	Lower-case R	(rolled R, none in English)
or [ɾ]	Fish-hook R	me<u>rr</u>y (formal, flipped R)
20. [p]	Lower-case P	<u>p</u>ie
21. [b]	Lower-case B	<u>b</u>uy
22. [t]	Lower-case T	<u>t</u>oo
23. [d]	Lower-case D	<u>d</u>o
24. [k]	Lower-case K	<u>c</u>ap
25. [g]	Lower-case G	<u>g</u>ap
26. [f]	Lower-case F	<u>f</u>at
27. [v]	Lower-case V	<u>v</u>at
28. [s]	Lower-case S	<u>S</u>ue
29. [z]	Lower-case Z	<u>z</u>oo
30. [ʃ]	Esh	<u>sh</u>oe
31. [ʒ]	Yogh	a<u>z</u>ure
32. [ç]	C cedilla	(none in English)
33. [j]	Curly-tail J	<u>y</u>es
34. [x]	Lower-case X	(none in English)
35. [h]	Lower-case H	<u>h</u>appy
36. [ts]	T-S ligature	si<u>ts</u>